Tales
from the Script

The Behind-the-Camera Adventures of a
TV Comedy Writer

by Gene Perret

Tales from the Script
© 2010 Gene Perret All rights reserved.

Published in the United States of America by:
Bear Manor Media
PO Box 71426
Albany, Georgia 31708
www.bearmanormedia.com

ISBN 1-59393-529-3

Book & cover design by Darlene Swanson of Van-garde Imagery, Inc. • www.van-garde.com

*For Ed Hercer, who helped tremendously
in getting these adventures started*

Contents

Foreword

Television seems to be an incredibly visible craft. The performers step onto a brilliantly lighted stage with the cameras focused on them. They sing, dance, act, tell jokes, and do it all not only for you, but right in your home. The celebrities are there for you to see and enjoy each week, sometimes even each night.

Yet the entertainment you see on your television screen is only the proverbial tip of the iceberg. That's the part of the production that is in front of the camera. Behind the camera are countless talented, devoted, dedicated people supporting both the show and the performer. There are set designers, who make the scenery colorful and attractive to the eye. There are makeup people, who try their darndest to make the celebrities look attractive to the eye. There are costume designers, lighting professionals, sound experts, electrical authorities, and technical wizards, who know which cables to connect and which buttons to push to magically transfer that stage action to your home TV. There are gifted musicians, choreographers, sound effects people, and a veritable army of others that I'm forgetting.

One group of behind-the-camera workers that no performer can dare to forget is the writers. These creative folks are the only ones who are greeted when they show up for work by a completely blank page. Their challenging chore is to fill that page with sparkling, inventive entertainment.

Gene Perret, began his television writing career on the staff of my variety show, *The Jim Nabors Hour.* He went on from there to work as a writer, head-writer, and producer for various television shows for the next three decades.

In this book, *Tales from the Script*, Gene paints a delightful picture of that part of television which is not so visible. It's the world of television, especially from the writing point of view, that happens out of range of the camera's lens.

In this book, you'll learn of the executive decisions that created some of the shows you've watched and enjoyed over the years. You'll discover how some of the comedy sketches you laughed at were born. In all frankness, the book also reveals how some of the comedy bits you never would have laughed at were mercifully cut from the shows before broadcast.

In these pages, you'll enjoy some of the camaraderie that made working on a television production so exciting. You'll also learn of some of the feuds that often made working on a television production almost unbearable.

Normally, all of us view television head-on. We face the screen and accept whatever the producers and directors of the various shows offer us. Gene's book is a more panoramic view of television production. It does include many of the on-screen shenanigans, but it also turns the camera to focus on the action behind it.

This book gives a much fuller picture of television production and entertainment. It begins with the blank pages, tells how the scripts were developed, rehearsed, and staged. It continues on through the broadcast and even to the eventual rave reviews or pans from the critics.

This is an invitation to sit in on the writers meetings and to be in the room as the jokes and sketches are being written. It's a VIP pass to stand on the stage, out of camera range, as the shows are rehearsed and taped.

I'm personally going to enjoy reading it because I'm eager to find out exactly what was going on around the studio while I was busy in wardrobe fittings and makeup.

Enjoy it.

Jim Nabors
July 13, 2009

Chapter One
The Moment of Conception

I was conceived in a public restroom. Not me, the person—me, the humorist. It happened in a restaurant in South Philadelphia when I was around six or seven years old.

I was combing my hair when two young sailors came into the men's room. One of them noticed the prominent cowlick on the back of my head. He touched it and said, "What's this?"

Talking to his image in the mirror, I said, "Oh, that's my personality."

They both laughed, but they did not just laugh; they got hysterical. What I said didn't seem that funny to me. Cute, I'll admit, but funny? They thought it was, though. It struck them just the right way and they couldn't stop laughing.

I liked that sound. Making people laugh like that thrilled me. A surge of power rushed through my innards. I felt like a genius at that moment, a comedy savant.

Deep inside my spirit, some comic spermatozoa penetrated an egg of humor and a gag writer was conceived.

Chapter Two
The Switchgear Friars

Some comedian once commented that a person goes into a life of comedy the same way that a woman might go into a life of sin. First they try it for the fun of it, then they start entertaining a few friends, and then they say, "What the hell, I might as well make a buck at it."

That's the way it happened for me.

Comedy had always intrigued me, so for the fun of it, I turned it into a hobby. During lunchtime chatter at work, I did little semi-rehearsed routines to get laughs from my colleagues. I cut pictures out of magazines, put captions on them, and pasted them in books to pass around to friends. I did cartoons about my family. I tried anything that would get laughs.

I wasn't the class clown. George Carlin gave the best explanation for that. He said he didn't have the courage to be the class clown, but he told the class clown what to do. That's the way I was—too shy to get up and perform comedy, but I loved writing it for others . . . until I went to work at General Electric's Switchgear Plant in southwest Philadelphia.

GE was hiring drafting apprentices—both mechanical and electrical, and I needed work. Since I was only eighteen-years old and knew nothing about electricity I applied for the position of mechanical drafting apprentice. However, GE administered a whole series of tests before hiring apprentices. My scores were high in all the exams except one—the interest test.

That dumb test posed questions like: If you were near a piano, would you

a) play it?

b) tune it?

c) try to fix it?

I didn't understand the rationale for most of the questions, so I simply wrote down whatever response occurred to me.

When the test results came in, the apprentice supervisor said, "You got magnificent scores in all your tests. Your mechanical interest, though, was rated a pitiable 10. Why don't you apply for electrical drafting?"

I said, "I don't know anything about electricity."

He said, "You're not very interested in mechanics."

I said, "But I don't know anything about electricity."

He said, "You'll either be hired as an electrical apprentice or you won't be hired at all."

I said, "I don't know anything about electricity, but I would like to be an electrical drafting apprentice."

I got the job and became an electrical drafting apprentice, albeit one who knew nothing about electricity. Later, GE promoted me to an electrical draftsman, then an electrical designer, then an electrical engineer, and eventually, an electrical drafting supervisor. I still knew nothing about electricity.

That supervisor who forced me into electrical work later unwittingly became a major factor in launching my career in an area that I did know something about.

He retired.

It was a tradition at that plant to throw a party for people retiring or celebrating twenty-five years with the company. Co-workers would organize the event and we'd all pay to attend. Part of the ticket price would go towards buying the guest of honor a gift from all of us.

When that gentleman retired, people, knowing my comedic passion, asked me to "do a little something" at the banquet.

He was the Supervisor of Apprentices, and all of his employees attended Drexel Institute of Technology. In the apprentice program, we worked a full forty-hour week and attended classes three evenings a week. So I wrote a little sketch about that man being the oldest student in Drexel.

It went over very well with the audience. People complimented me on the presentation and also suggested that I do something for Harry in Manufacturing, who was shortly to celebrate twenty-five years, or Charlie in the Sales Department, who was to retire in about a month, or Sylvia the Manager's secretary, who was to celebrate an anniversary. I did them all.

I quickly became the "Toastmaster General of General Electric," but only at that one plant and I gained a reputation as a witty emcee. I was like the Bob Hope, Johnny Carson, or Jay Leno of the Switchgear Plant.

My gags were always topical and usually about the guest of honor. If I didn't know the guest of honor well, I'd interview some of the people who did in order to gather research about him or her. When I had enough material to work with, I'd write about thirty to thirty-five gags about that person and that would become my eight to ten minute stint as the master of ceremonies. Here are a few samples:

There were two gentlemen in the drafting department, who worked on most projects as a team. Frank prided himself on his handyman capabilities. He was always refinishing a room or remodeling his house. Mike had a crew cut.

Frank was the guest of honor at one banquet, and I said, "Frank's a handyman with a hammer and a saw. You didn't think Mike went to a barber for those haircuts, did you?"

Another man celebrating a twenty-fifth anniversary with GE was a large man, noted for his loud, booming voice. I said about talking to him on the telephone, "He's the only man in the plant you can hang up on without losing volume."

Another gentleman had eight children and he always smoked a pipe. He was never without it and constantly fidgeting with it. I said at his banquet, "I spoke to his wife before the dinner and asked if it bothered her that her husband was always fiddling with that pipe. She said, "Not at all. After eight children, I'm for anything that keeps his hands busy."

Then, we had a gentleman who attended most of these affairs and always boasted of his drinking prowess. He didn't have a drinking problem (or I wouldn't have kidded him); he just liked to pretend he did. I went along with it by making him the butt of many of my jokes, such as these:

"Some people like Charlie's beard and others don't. I've got news for you. That's not really a beard. It's his breath running down his chin. Charlie visits Cavanaugh's (the local tavern across the street from the plant) so much that on his retirement Mr. Cavanaugh lit a perpetual flame in his honor. He set fire to Charlie's breath. In fact, Charlie and his friends stop at a lot of watering holes on their way home from work. You may call it the Baltimore Pike, but to them it's known as 'Chug-a-lug Trail.'"

That gentleman wore glasses constantly, but we all knew that at those parties, after his second drink, he'd take his glasses off and put them in his pocket. So I used that as fodder for one of my gags at his twenty-fifth anniversary party. I said, "We all know that after Charlie's had one or two drinks he takes his glasses off and puts them in his pocket. I spoke to his wife and said, 'I guess after nineteen years of marriage you always know when Charlie's been drinking whenever he comes home without his glass on.' She said, 'What glasses?'"

My comedy career had not yet hatched, but the following gag was particularly influential. I later reworked it and sold it as one of my first sales to Phyllis Diller. A very well-liked gentleman in the plant retired. He was a big man, weighing over 300 pounds. He didn't mind being kidded about his weight (I always checked on that because I never wanted any of the guests of honor to be offended by the comedy). So at his party, I said, "You know, I generally do these banquets for free, but tonight, Bill's going to give me the shirt he wore on his last day at work. I plan to have it starched and made into a summer home."

From the time I did that comedy skit for my first supervisor, all of the GE parties became "roasts." We kidded the guest of honor just as the show business Friars did when they honored one of their members. I and a few of the others who were willing to stand at the microphone and make presentations became known as "The Switchgear Friars."

Emceeing a retirement party for The Switchgear Friars

Everything I have accomplished and enjoyed in comedy writing is due to the support and the encouragement of my co-workers and management at GE's Switchgear Plant in Philadelphia.

The folks appreciated and looked forward to our shenanigans at those parties. The guest of honor generally asked for a copy of the script as a keepsake. It was through word of mouth from GE colleagues that I landed my first writing contracts with Slappy White and then with Phyllis Diller. Slappy was a well-known black comedian who, like many of his colleagues at that time, was making the transition into the white clubs. Both Slappy and Phyllis heard about my material from people who worked at General Electric.

It was a great training ground for my comedy writing for many reasons.

1) The audience was appreciative and very receptive. They came to know me and my comedy style and they liked it. However, they were also demanding. They expected quality. They liked to laugh and they wanted good gags to laugh at. Consequently, they were a good comedy barometer.

2) I did so many of those affairs that I began to learn which style of gag would work and which would not. It's something that many professional writers spend years learning.

3) I began to appreciate the importance of characterizations. I learned that each performer has a personality, a style, a character. Bob Hope can't do a Bill Cosby joke, and Bill can't do a Hope joke (I was reminded of this years later when I worked for both of them.). I began to take on a persona as the emcee at these banquets. Bob Hope was the overriding influence on my comedy writing and delivery. One time, though, I tried to change my technique. I did a banquet in a

Jackie Leonard fashion. Leonard was a very funny insult comedian, similar in style to Don Rickles. I stood at the microphone and insulted the audience. As soon as I began, I knew it was wrong. People weren't so much offended, because they knew I was kidding, but they were confused. I could almost see the question on their faces: Where are your regular jokes? People told me afterwards that the stuff was funny, but it wasn't me. That was a very important lesson for a young comedy writer to learn.

4) Those shows taught me that one has to work at comedy. It should look easy and inspired, but it can only look that way if you spend hours writing the material and rehearsing it. Again, those people began to expect quality. They wanted the phrasing of the gags to be just right and they wanted them to roll off the tongue. At the same time, they had to appear as if I was just thinking that stuff up on the spot. That takes effort. Again, not a bad habit for an aspiring comedy writer to acquire.

5) Those banquets taught me respect for the performer. Many writers felt their words are sacrosanct, untouchable. I was both the writer and the performer at those affairs. I knew that the performer wanted to get laughs regardless of the writer's feelings. That helped me tremendously when I began writing professionally for others. I'd listen to their input rather than

insisting, "My stuff's funny—just do it as written." When I work today with young writers, I always recommend that they try delivering their own material. Even if they don't want to be standup comedians, I suggest they give it a try. Whether they're a smash or a flop, they will learn something from the experience.

6) Another insight I gained from those shows was the emotional pitfalls of being an entertainer. I appreciated better the problems they might have despite their wealth and fame. I was something of a celebrity at those small affairs. People wanted to hear my monologues and they laughed and applauded for me. It was exhilarating. Then after the shows were over, I'd go back to just being one of their co-workers again. Folks had a drink with their close friends and I was no longer the center of attention. Sometimes, that was demoralizing and it helped me later to understand why certain well-known performers could sometimes be moody.

I also came to appreciate the power of humor. Aside from the fact that people wanted me to entertain at every party, luncheon, or dinner that was connected with the people who worked there, other good things happened for me. For instance, when promotions were available, my name was often mentioned because people knew me; they knew my name. I didn't always get the job, but I was in the running.

When I finally did get a supervisory job, I saw again the power of humor. The plant was experiencing some labor problems. Management and the Union were negotiating, but it wasn't going well. A strike seemed imminent and the materials published by both sides were acutely accusatory.

I was at the lowest rung of the management team, yet the brass invited me into the strategy sessions. I asked our top manager why. He said, "We can tell from your humor that you know what the people are thinking. That's why we want your input."

I was flattered, astounded, and awed by the power of comedy.

Unfortunately, I also learned during that time the danger of humor. Both management and the work force attended those parties. There was no discrimination because we all attended not as bosses or employees; we went there as friends of the guest of honor. Much of my material dealt with work-related topical matters, events that were happening in the offices and the factories where we worked.

One time, I kidded about a large blueprint machine on the third floor that was troublesome. I said, "It serves a good purpose in engineering. It eats harmful drawings." It was funny stuff and it went over well because everyone knew that the machine needed work.

After the dinner, one of the supervisors came over to me and said, "You just ruined my career."

I said, "What?"

He said, "I'm responsible for that machine. It's my job to keep it operating. Thanks for embarrassing me in front of my managers."

I don't think his fears were justified. The management team was too smart to take my comments that seriously, but his disappointment in me was justified.

I learned then, and I hope I still remember today, that comedy has a cutting edge to it. It can be harmful if not used properly and wisely.

From then on, whenever I wrote material about a guest of honor, I always checked it over with a few of his or her close friends. If they felt it might be misconstrued or offensive, I replaced the gag. My philosophy remained: If in doubt, cut it out.

Those were all lessons I learned as part of my unofficial comedy writing apprenticeship at General Electric, but I learned other things there that had nothing to do with comedy. Strangely, though, they were beneficial as my career progressed.

One day, a group of us in the office was playing around with a test that was printed in the Sunday paper magazine supplement. It was a complicated challenge, but interesting. It consisted of a series of about seventy-two words printed in different colored inks. The words were all colors. So, the word "blue" might be printed in red ink; the word "green" might be in blue ink, and so on. The object of the test was to name the colors of the inks as quickly as you could. The challenge, of course, was that you were looking at two colors at the same time—the written word and the color of the ink. It took concentration to keep focused on only one of them as you read the list. Someone would time you and then the article would tell you how you scored and what it proved.

I read the test in a certain amount of time and the test stated that I was careless. I disputed that. My friends said, "Well, when you go that fast, you obviously make several mistakes."

I said, "I didn't make any mistakes." (Have I mentioned that I was also a cocky son of a gun?)

One gentleman said, "Do it again and I'll check your results as you go."

So, I started reading off the colors. He stopped me and said, "You made three mistakes on that line alone." He pointed to the line he was referring to.

I said, "I'm not on that line. I'm on the next one."

He said, "Well, I was watching and I had you on this line."

I wanted to know how he could check the accuracy of my answers when I could read the colors faster than he did.

To help settle the dispute, a co-worker suggested that someone write out the correct answers on a sheet of paper and use that to check my reading. They did and I made no errors and still maintained the original speed.

That was just a simple parlor game in a Sunday magazine supplement. It proved nothing, really. However, it did teach me a lesson—that no one could effectively judge my work except me. It was tremendously valuable for an aspiring writer to realize because much writing was rejected. Often, it was rejected by people who didn't have nearly the same amount of talent. A writer can't just accept any person's opinion. They have to know the critic's background and experience, and they have to maintain confidence in their own judgment and ability.

That works the other way, too. A novel may not become a best seller just because our Aunt Matilda thinks it's better than *Gone with the Wind*. Aunt Matilda may not know as much about the publishing business as the folks who sent your manuscript back to you with a polite rejection letter.

My work experience at GE served me well as a writer, also. One of my assignments was to take the plant's engineering logic and condense it into a package that could be put into the computer. I had to analyze every aspect of our engineering logic. Much of comedy writing is analytical. The writer has to ask many questions about the topic. What's connected with it? What does it affect? How do people respond? What's funny about the topic? Learning to pull subjects apart, as I did as part of my job description, proved beneficial when I turned to professional comedy writing.

People don't always say what they mean. In fact, people don't always know what they mean. When I did have to analyze the engineering logic, I didn't know what the engineering logic was. I had to interview the engineers. Of course, they all told me that I couldn't take that knowledge and put it into a computer because it was too extensive; it was a people process and not a computer process.

I told them I realized that, but it was my job. I said, "If you had the job of putting that logic into a computer, how would you go about it?" They told me exactly how to do it. Even though they insisted it couldn't be done, they told me how to do it. Realizing that people don't know what they mean or don't say what they mean can be helpful in dealing with producers and studio executives.

At General Electric, I learned to be patient and to trust that things would happen when they were ready to happen. Young writers are impatient. We all want to sell an Academy Award-winning screenplay before we learn how to structure a story.

I had that problem as a young electrical apprentice. Our superiors told us that we were the ones who would be the supervisors of tomorrow. I was skeptical of the rosy future they were painting for us. I thought to myself, "Yeah, sure." I was certain they were telling that to us just so we'd apply ourselves and work extra hard for some pie-in-the-sky, never-to-be-delivered promise.

A few short years later, several of our apprentices were supervisors, including me.

Then, I realized what a dummy I was for being so mistrusting. *I shouldn't be so cynical about the writing profession,* I thought. *Be patient. Let the skills mature. Think positively about the future. Good things will happen when they happen.*

Robert Benchley once admitted, "I took me fifteen years to discover that I had no talent for writing, but I couldn't give it up because by that time I was too famous."

So, as a young apprentice at General Electric, I began to learn the craft and business of comedy writing. It was more my fault than the company's, but after thirteen years at the plant, I still didn't know much about electricity.

Chapter Three
The Early Years

To paraphrase Charles Dickens, being a wannabe writer was the best of times and the worst of times. It was the best of times because I had no demanding deadlines to meet since no one had hired me to write anything. I was never behind because I had nothing to do. It was a pleasant time because no one was looking over my shoulder second guessing everything I did. No one was demanding rewrites that insulted my sensitivities. In fact, no one gave a damn what I wrote. It was a glorious time because I could declare myself the greatest gag-writer in the world and no one contradicted me. They didn't say my material wasn't the greatest because they never saw any of my material. No one had seen it—except me.

It was the worst of times because I seemed to be going nowhere. No one wanted to buy my stuff; no one wanted to see my stuff. "Why should I bother to look at your stuff?" they said.

I said, "Because I'm a great comedy writer."

They said, "If you were any good, I would've heard of you by now."

That came from comedians that I had never heard of.

One rebuke literally came from a comedian that no one had ever heard of. I used to scan the local papers and search out comics who were playing the clubs in the area, and then I'd call them, tell them I wrote great material, and see if I could arrange a meeting to discuss a contract.

I called one club and asked to speak to the comedian whose name I've forgotten. When he got on the telephone, I said, "I'm a comedy writer and I think I have some material that could help your act."

He said, "Who's this?"

I said, "Gene Perret."

He said, "I never heard of you."

I said, "But I have some great material that I think can help your act."

He said, "Have you seen my act?"

I said, "No, but some of my friends saw you work before and they told me that my material is perfectly suited for your act."

He said, "That's interesting, because this is the first job I've ever had as a comedian."

I said, "I wish you luck in your career," and hung up.

That's how I spent the early years of my writing career—hustling, trying to con comics into looking at my stuff, and scheming to get them to part with a few bucks for a few jokes. Parting with a few bucks was not one of their favorite pastimes.

One local performer, who used to do an act with his brother, was then doing a single act. Somehow, a friend of his knew a friend of mine that knew I did a little comedy writing, so a meeting was arranged either by the performer, the friend of his, the friend of mine, or me. I forget who.

I arrived at the small club where the comic was working. It was actually a bar in South Philadelphia. The only person in the place when I arrived was the bartender. I told him I was looking for the comedian scheduled to perform that evening.

"I'll get him," the bartender volunteered.

The comic came out, we exchanged pleasantries, and then he told me exactly what sort of material he was looking for. I showed him my pages and he laughed at a couple of the gags.

Then, the bartender came over and interrupted.

"Would you guys like something to drink?" he said?

I said, "Yes. I'll have a scotch on the rocks and . . . ." I turned to the comic to see if he would like to join me, but he was either gone, had disappeared, or had dematerialized.

The bartender brought two drinks. I paid for them and started to sip mine, but then my comic friend reappeared and said, "Yeah, I like some of these jokes, but you really should see my act." We discussed his wants and needs for a while.

When our glasses were near empty, the bartender came back.

"Another round?" he asked.

I said, "Yeah, I'll have the same and . . . ."

The comic was gone again.

Two more drinks came. I paid for them, and then the comedian reappeared.

Every time drinks had to be paid for, that guy evaporated—and took his wallet with him.

Eventually, he got on stage to perform. The bartender and I were still the only people in the room. Nevertheless, the comedian did his act full out and I continued to pay for my own drinks.

Then, another couple came into the club—a young lady and her drunken escort. They sat close to the stage and she kept loudly telling him how drunk he was, and he kept loudly telling the comedian how unfunny he was.

When the show mercifully ended, the comic and I talked again.

He said, "How about that, huh? There are only four people in the room and I get a heckler."

I said, "Well, I could write some good lines for you to use against hecklers."

He said, "Yeah, I'd like that. Hey, by the way, would you like a drink?"

I didn't really want one, but I accepted the offer. I was determined that the cheapskate would pay for something.

He turned towards the bar and said, "Hey, Charlie . . . ." That time, the bartender disappeared. Those two worked together better than Abbot and Costello.

We sat there without drinks and he said, "I like your stuff. I want you to write for me."

I was thrilled. I started to say, "My fees are . . . ."

He said, "I can't really pay for material right now, but I'll tell you what. You write something that'll get me on *The Tonight Show* and I'll send you a few bucks."

If this guy ever mails me a check, I thought to myself, *my mailman would dematerialize.* He was strictly a "no sale."

That was the frustration of trying to make enough money to justify the time I spent writing jokes. Comedians often spent a tiny fortune for a great looking tuxedo with piping on the lapels and pockets. They'd gladly shell out an exorbitant amount for patent leather shoes to wear only on stage. They'd pay greens fees to play golf everyday because that's what the classy performers like Dean Martin and Bob Hope did, but they had no money to pay for jokes.

So, I pursued the ones that had money. I wrote letters to, placed phone calls to, and practically stalked any "name" comedians playing in local clubs.

At that time, Vaughn Meader was an impersonator hitting it big with his album called *The First Family,* a take-off on President John F. Kennedy and his family. Vaughn did a magnificent impression of Kennedy. After the album went to the top of the charts, Meader was booked into high-priced clubs. When he came to the Latin Casino outside of Philadelphia, I was on the phone to him.

He agreed to meet me in his motel room before the show. As he politely read over my samples, I worked up the courage to point out one particular joke to him. "I did this joke in a talk I gave last week and it was the biggest laugh in my whole routine."

"Well, it wouldn't be the biggest laugh in my act," he said.

If you're interested in sainthood and would like to master the virtue of humility, consider becoming a comedy writer, especially one who leads with his chin like I did with that idiotic straight line.

Meader finished reading my material and didn't seem overwhelmed or even whelmed.

He said, "There's not much Kennedy stuff in here."

I said, "No, I do a lot of topical material, but you know you can't do Kennedy forever."

He dismissed me after that impolitic statement, but I was right. He didn't do Kennedy impersonations much longer.

London Lee was a young comic making a big splash on *The Ed Sullivan Show.* London was a variation of Jerry Lewis, although he did mostly one-liners as opposed to Jerry's physical shtick. His underlying premise was that he was rich. His dad was a successful businessman and London grew up with money.

When he was booked into New Jersey's Latin Casino, he discovered I came with the terrain. That time, though, I was smarter. I wrote material that was particularly suited to London Lee's act. He had been on television quite a bit, so I got to know the kinds of gags he was doing.

Several people were in his dressing room when we met. I introduced myself, but he didn't introduce me to the others. He took my pages of gags and retreated into his private dressing room along with all those other people. I sat in the anteroom for about an hour. When London Lee came back out, he said, "There are some good jokes here."

I was delighted.

"But I'm not going to buy any of them," he said.

I was undelighted.

"Do you know why?" he asked. Before I could answer, he explained. "Because I'm already doing them."

I traveled home disappointed and confused. Not only did he declare me an incompetent, but also a plagiarist. When I wasn't busy feeling sorry for myself, I wondered why, if he was already doing those jokes, it took him an hour to read them.

The next time I saw London Lee on television, he did a few of my lines, which, of course, he claimed were already his lines. I suppose by then they were.

I came closer with Henny Youngman. He was scheduled to do a private banquet at some Philadelphia hotel. When I found out about it, I gathered my pages of sample jokes and planted myself outside the ballroom. So did another writer whom I didn't know.

When Youngman showed up, we both swooped down on him like stereo stalkers. Youngman was gracious, though. He said, "C'mon, we'll sit down for a few minutes and you can read me some of your stuff."

The other writer was much more gregarious than I was. He was a big mouth, and he wasn't really a writer; he was a borrower. He started reading one of his jokes and Youngman read him the punch line. He'd begin another gag and Youngman finished it. The same thing happened with the third joke.

Finally, Youngman said, "I don't have time to listen to jokes I heard forty years ago," and left.

That time, I was rejected simply because I happened to be in the vicinity of a very bad writer.

For a while, I seriously considered beginning a new hobby—collecting interesting rejections. I had an extensive assortment. They poured in from magazines, book publishers, agents, and comics. Practically anyone who could say "no" to me did.

The one from Joe E. Lewis was my favorite. I'd written to him and offered to send along a few pages of sample gags if he was interested in seeing them. Lewis wrote back to me on a small note pad from the Fountainbleu Hotel in Florida. It read, "I already have a writer. Joe E. Lewis."

All those rejections could have been demoralizing to an aspiring, young comedy writer, but they weren't. English poet Thomas Gray once remarked, "Ignorance is bliss." I was so blissfully ignorant at that stage that I thought I was not only the best comedy writer in the world, but the only one. Well, at least the only really good one.

I believe I did mention earlier that I was cocky. When those folks turned me down, I actually felt sorry for them. *Boy, did they miss out on a great opportunity,* I thought. That's cocky.

I was so cocky that if the man I was then could have come to the man I became later and asked for advice, I'd throw the man I was then out on his ass. So, in the midst of all that disappointment, my future continued to look promising, but it also continued to remain in the future. Not too much rewarding or profitable was happening in the present,

Also during that time, the true secret of success manifested itself to me. There's a truism that applies to comedy writing, the legal profession, car sales, or any line of business, and it is to have a friend who has a friend who has a friend who knows somebody.

Since people in the comedy profession wouldn't buy my material, I decided to buy it myself. I became a performer and planned to get rich as a comedy writer selling jokes to myself. There was a flaw in the logic of that strategy, but I was too blind with ambition to notice it at the time.

There was a private club in our area that periodically featured entertainment. I had a friend who had a friend who had a friend who knew the General Manager of that club, the Drexelbrook. One of those friends in the previous sentence arranged an audition for me.

Telling jokes in front of an audience of strangers was a frightening experience. Telling gags to an audience of one was terrifying, but I did it, and I did it half well. The general manager liked my jokes, but he wasn't sold on my delivery. Nevertheless, he gave me a break. He let me perform, without pay of course, at the club. However, he wouldn't let me perform in the main room. I was relegated to the rowdy downstairs room.

On the night of the show, that same gentleman introduced me like this: "Ladies and gentlemen, we have something special for you tonight. This young man came to me and asked if I could give him his first break as a comedian. I thought he was funny, but needed a lot of work. And so I invited him here tonight to entertain you with some funny stories and jokes. He's only a beginner and, as I said, he needs a lot of work, but I knew you folks would be kind to him. So why don't you give him a break. Gene Perret."

I died that night, but blamed it on the audience and the introduction. There was no way that it could it have been my fault.

So, I had another friend who had a friend who had a friend who knew someone who was putting together a show for the Knights of Columbus. They hired me, for no money of course, to be the emcee and comedian for the evening at one of their social events.

I was a smash.

That crowd laughed and applauded. Together, we even created a little catch phrase for the evening. After one joke, some lady in the audience cackled after the general laughter died down. I remarked to her, "You, too, lady?" That got giant laughs, so I used it several times throughout my performance.

After the show ended and the serious drinking, dancing, and partying began, I heard people shouting that phrase back and forth to one another and laughing. I was thrilled that I had created a "catch phrase."

It was a glorious evening. The audience loved the performance, and the people who put on the show booked me immediately for another one a month later—at the same fee.

That time, I wanted people to share my exultation, so I invited my wife and her mother to be my guests.

I died.

Not even "You, too, lady?" worked. No one laughed and the applause was polite and peremptory. It said, "Get off the stage so we can get on with our party" more than it said, "Thanks for an enjoyable show."

Afterward, I learned that one of the Philadelphia college basketball teams, either St. Joseph's or Villanova, was playing for the national championship that night and management had set up several televisions around the room so the party-goers could watch the game.

Again, it wasn't my fault.

Another friend had a friend who had a friend who knew someone at WFIL-TV, who was organizing several traveling amateur troupes sponsored by the station. One of those friends got me information about applying for an audition.

Everyone in the Philadelphia area must have had a friend who had a friend who had a friend because there were hundreds of hopefuls lining the corridors of WFIL-TV on tryout day. There were little girls in tutus, who danced by on their tippy-toes, while I sat on a folding chair rehearsing my gags. It reminded me of some comedian's line, "Why do ballet dancers stand on their tippy-toes? Why don't they just hire taller girls?"

There were several youngsters in ill-fitting tuxedos with colored scarves protruding from every pocket. They were the magicians, and they paced back and forth because if they sat down, they'd probably kill a dove that was secreted in their back pocket.

Some young ladies rehearsed their Joan of Arc soliloquies, sang operatic arias in a near whisper, or tapped away in their red, white, and blue sailor suits. It was probably the greatest assemblage of non-talent and semi-talent in the Delaware Valley. I was awed to be a part of it.

Memorizing my lines distracted me from the chaos in the corridor. My eyes and my mind stayed focused on my script until I heard a barking coming from somewhere near me. I ignored it at first, but the second time I heard the noise, I looked up.

The older gentleman next to me smiled proudly and said, "Cocker Spaniel."

I said, "Oh," and went back to my private rehearsal.

"Here's a German Shepherd," he said and barked again. It sounded a lot like a Cocker Spaniel only louder. Without comment, I returned to my reading. He tugged at my sleeve and said, "Here's a Cocker Spaniel and a German Shepherd fighting." The noises emanating from that man turned many heads. One tuxedoed lad reacted quite strongly when the barking and growling scared a dove that was hidden in his pocket.

My new friend proudly said, "I can do a rooster," and he did. He said, "I can do a cat," and he did. He even boasted, "I can do a cat falling from a building," and he did. I had never heard a cat falling from a building, but I supposed if I had it would've sounded just like that man. The young magician had probably never heard a cat falling from a building either and I'm sure that none of his doves ever had. The magician had to go into the men's room at the end of the corridor because his tuxedo was becoming very active.

"I'm an animal impersonator," my seat mate finally said.

"Really?" I asked, as if I needed confirmation that a man who just barked several times, meowed, squealed, and cock-a-doodle-dooed would be anything other than an animal impersonator.

"Oh yeah," he said. I got my confirmation.

He said, "I do over 400 different types of animals." I hoped my name would be called before he got past number 166.

"I was on the Ted Mack Amateur Hour, you know."

I didn't know that and told him so.

"Yeah, but they put me on New Year's Eve." He was obviously annoyed at that. "Who watches on New Year's Eve?"

I withdrew into my own fantasy for my own amusement and to shut out the noises coming out of that man's mouth as he did his act, "Animals from A to Z." He started with the aardvark.

My mind began to imagine what would've happened if he'd been given a shot on Ted Mack's show on a night with more viewers. He would've been a smash. He would've gone on to great heights. I pictured him opening in Las Vegas in a glitzy tuxedo, wowing the audience. I fantasized about him taking a breather from the performance—somewhere between the Hippopotamus and the Iguana—sipping a little bit of scotch like Dean Martin, unloosening his tie like Sammy Davis, and hearing his adoring fans shout out requests.

"Do the porcupine sliding along an icy road," one would yell.

"Do the impersonation of the elephant impersonating Jimmy Durante," another hollered.

"I'll do them all folks. You ain't heard nothing, yet," that master showman would reply.

Then, someone called my name and released me from my reverie. I shook hands with the impersonator and wished him luck in his career. He whimpered and rubbed up against my leg. "Miniature poodle," he said.

I hastened in to my audition—and I died. I wasn't assigned to any of the traveling troupes. Once again, it wasn't my fault. I would've been great if I hadn't been distracted by the Rich Little of the Animal World.

One person was impressed with my performance, though. It was an aspiring singer, who thought we could do an act together. "With my voice and your comic talents we'd be great. We'd be another Martin and Lewis," he said.

Finally, someone recognizes great talent! Except for the billing, which should have been, "With your comic talents and my voice," I agreed with everything he said.

So we teamed up. I wrote a Martin and Lewis type of act. It

opened with him singing "Put On a Happy Face," and from there on, it was hilarious mayhem. His voice was not that great, but it didn't matter. The comedy was brilliant enough to overcome that slight flaw, just like Jerry Lewis had remarkably carried Dean Martin.

That time, my partner had a friend who had a friend who had a friend who knew a guy who owned a club. One of those friends got us booked into the club on a Saturday night—for no money, of course.

One night, my partner and I sat in my kitchen planning how we would approach our theatrical debut. I said, "I usually like to work in a tuxedo."

My wife, who was preparing some snacks or something in the kitchen at the time observed, "What do you mean 'usually'? You've never worked before." We agreed that business suits, which we wouldn't have to rent, would be sufficient.

Remembering the Knights of Columbus fiasco, I didn't invite anyone to the opening. My singing friend, though, invited several.

When we got to the club, we saw that it was just a tiny little bar on the outskirts of the outskirts of Philadelphia. A three-piece combo was seated behind the bar playing to three patrons in the bar, counting the one who had his head on the bar and was taking a nap.

I wrote a big act with enough action and motion to fill a Las Vegas stage. It required a stage larger than that entire bar, and it wasn't going to work.

"Let's just call this a bad idea," I told my partner.

He said, "What are you talking about? When the band takes a break, we'll rehearse with them and then we're on."

We rehearsed with the band and then we were on stage.

The stage was the bar itself. It was a long, elliptical bar. The two awake patrons and one comatose patron sat facing the far wall, where the other end of the ellipse was. The band sat behind the bar and we worked on the bar.

Fortunately, the singer opened the act. The bartender introduced him to the three patrons. The "voice" part of our tandem climbed onto the bar and actually straddled the cash register while performing. The band started playing "Put on a Happy Face," and my partner started crooning. At rehearsals, he was fine, but in front of an audience, stage fright got him. He sang the entire song using only one note.

During the song, the bartender rang up drinks on the cash register that was between the singer's legs. I sat at the end of the bar wondering if my whole show business career would be that bizarre.

God bless him, my partner continued singing as if he was Dean Martin. I just stared at him with wide open eyes, unbelieving. I had never heard anything so awful in my life.

At the end of his song, the microphone disassembled and fell with a loud clunk onto the stage. The bartender tried to fix it, but couldn't, so he said, "Just tell me what you want to say and I'll tell the people."

He told the bartender to announce me. He did. I refused to get off my bar stool. Our debut was over.

Again, I died, but that time I blamed it on my faux-Dean Martin associate and on the room. No matter what my wife said, we would have been better in tuxedos.

Some good things happened along the way, too. A friend had a friend who had a friend who knew Cozy Morley. Well, in fact, everybody knew Cozy Morley. He was an entertainer, who was very popular in the Philadelphia and Wildwood areas. He sang, played instruments, and told jokes, but the real secret of his success was that he knew everyone by name. He owned a club in the Wildwood area where he entertained during the summer season. He learned the name of anyone who came into the club and remembered it the following summer when they came back. Everybody flocked to see Cozy because he was a personal friend.

He read some of my jokes and wanted me to write material for him. Cozy had been doing the same jokes since he was in high school, so he wanted some new ones.

We settled on a fee of $100 a week. That was the first money I earned as a comedy writer, so I couldn't really afford a lawyer. I drew up the contract myself, and it was easy. Cozy was the party of the first part and I was the party of the second part, or visa versa. It didn't really matter.

I threw in a whole bunch of "whereases" and "wherefors" and used a big word anytime I could think of one to replace a little word. The document appeared legal and we both signed it.

After that, the document just withered away as did the agreement. Cozy never did any of the new jokes because the old ones were much more comfortable for him. I never saw any of the $100s I was supposed to receive each week. We both just forgot about it.

However, another friend had a friend who had a friend who personally knew Mickey Shaughnessy. That friend used to work with Mickey around town. Shaughnessy was another local favorite, who had recently had some success in Hollywood. He appeared in *From Here to Eternity* and in several Glenn Ford pictures like *Pocketful of Miracles* and the *Sheepherder*.

Mickey read my stuff and liked it. He immediately hired me to write some special material for a show he was going to do in Cleveland. I'd get $100 for my work.

I was thrilled.

Then Shaughnessy cancelled the appearance.

I was unthrilled.

However, he did want to meet me. He was appearing at the Venus Lounge in South Philadelphia. He invited me to see his act and then we could sit and talk about a working arrangement.

The day of the meeting, I was ill. I had a severely upset stomach, but I didn't want to miss that opportunity. I talked a good friend from GE into accompanying me. Actually, I talked him into taking me there because I was too ill to drive.

We sat in the audience, while Shaughnessy performed. My friend drank bourbon and I drank Pepto Bismol. I had thought to bring a bottle with me.

We talked to Mickey after the show and he was very enthusiastic about my material. I set up another meeting, this one at my house. Shaughnessy was going to come and have a spaghetti dinner with my family, and then we would finalize our comedian-writer relationship.

He cancelled that meeting, too.

I never really did write a line or make one penny from Mickey Shaughnessy, but he was influential in the development of my career. He recommended me and my work to Rex Morgan.

Rex Morgan was a local TV personality, who had a morning show on WFIL-TV. Shaughnessy showed him some of my jokes and recommended me as a writer. Morgan called me and invited me into a taping of his show, and then he asked me to write some topical lines for him to use. I wrote for him for about two weeks—for no money, of course. That was an audition again.

Morgan took my lines to his bosses at the station and asked for a salary for me as a regular writer for his show. The brass turned him, and me, down. "They said if they give me money for a writer, all the people here will want writers," Morgan explained to me.

So, that gig fell through.

However, Rex Morgan wanted to use my material to initiate a column in the *Philadelphia Inquirer*, the city's morning paper. He planned to call it "Over a Second Cup of Coffee" by Rex Morgan. I wouldn't get credit, but I'd probably get a little bit of money.

The *Philadelphia Inquirer* wasn't interested.

Rex Morgan had a guest on his morning show, who happened to read some of my material upside down while it sat on Morgan's desk. He was a comedian, who was always looking for good writers. He asked Morgan if he would contact me.

Morgan called me, and on the telephone, introduced me to a comedian named Slappy White, but I don't think we had a real good connection.

Slappy said, "I like the stuff you wrote and I'd like you to write for me."

"Great," I said.

Slappy said, "Can you meet me at my hotel and we'll talk about the material?"

"Sure," I said.

So we set up the meeting, and in closing, Slappy said, "Oh, and by the way, my name's 'Slappy,' not 'Sloppy.'" I had been calling him "Sloppy" throughout our phone conversation.

We did meet, though, and we did agree to a contract, but a less formal one than the one I wrote for Cozy Morley. We did work together.

At last, I got my revenge against all the rejections I'd received. I could tell Vaughn Meader, London Lee, WFIL-TV, the Drexelbrook Inn, and all the others to go to hell. I didn't need them anymore. I was now a professional comedy writer, pulling down a hefty $30 a week. Finally, I had gotten to the "What the hell, I might as well make a buck at it" phase of my career.

Chapter Four
Slappy White and Phyllis Diller

When people discover I write comedy, they usually say, "Say some-thing funny." When they do, I take out a pad, a pen, and say, "All right, who do I send the bill to?" Professional comedy writers get paid for writing gags. My personal definition of a joke is that it's "a series of words that ends in a paycheck."

The first joke I sold was to *Parade*, a magazine that came each week as part of our Sunday paper. The joke read: "There's no such thing as a Sunday driver anymore. They're all Friday drivers still look-ing for a parking space."

The check was nice, but the big thrill was that the gag was printed on a page facing a big article about Bob Hope, my idol. The gods of comedy seemed to be dropping me a prophetic hint. At least, I took it that way.

Cash was a powerful incentive. Jokes began to flow more regu-larly once I learned that people would pay for them. At that time, *Kiplinger Magazine* used to feature a page of topical one-liners called "Changing Times." They began accepting my submissions regularly and paying $5 a joke.

Slappy White, though (That's "Slappy," not "Sloppy") was my first official contract in Show Biz. Mickey Shaughnessy was the first who was going to hire me, but he never actually did. No money ever changed hands. Since, by my definition, a joke is a series of words that ends in a paycheck, I never really wrote any jokes for Mickey Shaughnessy.

The contract I had with Cozy Morley was a faux document. It was a quasi-legal agreement that I wrote myself. Whereas the party of the first part never did any of the jokes that were written by the party of the second part, and whereas the party of the second part doesn't remember ever receiving a check from the party of the first part, be it therefore understood that this agreement hereto didn't amount to a hill of beans.

Slappy's contract, though, was legit. Slappy was a black comedian, who had been in show business most of his life. He was once the partner of Redd Foxx. With the emergence on television of other black comedians, notably Dick Gregory and Godfrey Cambridge, black comics were being integrated into the white nightclubs. Slappy wanted fresh, topical material to capitalize on that.

After that phone call from Rex Morgan's office, I wrote some audition material for an appearance Slappy had in a Philadelphia night club. Hot topics at the time were the new movie, *Cleopatra*, and the scandal involving the stars, Richard Burton, Liz Taylor, and her husband Eddie Fisher. One joke I did for Slappy was about the low-cut costume Liz Taylor wore in the film. He said, "I went to see that movie, *Cleopatra*, the other night. The man behind me kept saying, 'I never saw anything like that before. I never saw anything like that before.' I turned around. It was Eddie Fisher. The man next to me said, 'I have.' It was Richard Burton."

Another big movie then was *Lawrence of Arabia*. For Slappy I wrote: "I went to see that movie, *Lawrence of Arabia*, too, but I couldn't enjoy it. I can't enjoy any movie that has that many people running around in white sheets. No sir, I get nervous when I see two or three Good Humor men hanging around together."

According to our agreement, I'd supply jokes to Slappy on a regular basis and he'd pay me 5% of whatever salary he earned as a comedian. Faithfully, Slappy sent me the AGVA (American Guild of Variety Artists) contracts for his various engagements, and just as faithfully, he sent my cut. I was now a professional earning about $1,500 a year from my joke writing. I was in Show Business. I was making money from writing jokes. I was happy. Slappy was an ideal partner. He listed my name in any ads he took out in the papers— "Special Material by Gene Perret." What an ego boost.

Slappy always praised the good material and ignored the bad. Once, I auditioned for another comedian at the same time I was writing for Slappy. This comic called and complained bitterly about the thirty-joke routine I had sent him. "There're only two gags in that whole batch you sent me that I could use. You sent me thirty jokes and I only liked two of them. You expect me to pay money for three pages of material when I can only use two? The next batch had better be a lot better if you want to write for me."

Then, Slappy called. "Hey, two of those jokes you sent me worked beautifully. They got screams. Do a couple more like that, will you?"

Naturally, I went to work writing more jokes for Slappy and never wrote another word for whatshisname.

Slappy even paid my expenses periodically to come see his act and hang around with him backstage at the Playboy Clubs. Once, he

Slappy White (on the left) and former Heavyweight Champion
Joe Louis at the Club Harlem in Atlantic City

flew me to Boston to catch his act at a club in nearby Revere Beach.
Between acts, he told me to take his car and go to another club to
catch the comedy team of Reese and Martin. "See what kind of stuff
they're doing and how well they're going over."

Slappy drove a brand new, top of the line Cadillac. I was driving a
twelve-year-old Buick at the time that usually required a screwdriver
to help it get started. In the club parking lot, I started the Caddy,
but didn't know how to release the emergency brake. I pushed a but-
ton and the outside mirrors started readjusting themselves. I pulled
something else and the windshield wipers sprayed water and started
clacking back and forth. The more buttons I pushed and pulled, the
more things happened in the car. The radio went on, the windows

went up and down, the heater blew harder, but the emergency brake never did release. Finally, I decided that it wasn't my car, so I'd drive to the other club with the emergency brake on. When I shifted into gear, the emergency brake pedal released.

Another time, Slappy, a dancer from the show, and I sat in a coffee shop in St. Louis at about two o'clock in the morning. We were having a cup of coffee after the show and before retiring to our rooms. The place was pretty much deserted except for one other gentleman, who apparently had over-indulged. He marched over to our table and stood there while we conversed. Finally, he said, "We don't allow negroes in here."

We stopped in there each night after the show and we were welcomed by the management. That particular drunk had his own agenda, but it frightened me. I was prepared for serious trouble.

It didn't bother Slappy, though. He casually looked up at this gentleman and said, "I'm an American Indian."

The guy said, "Oh, that's OK, then," and walked away.

Slappy White was a master at comedian-writer relationships. He kept me enthused and excited about writing. He even gave me a taste of performing.

Together, we created a routine where Slappy White was the first black man to run for President. As a supposed candidate, he held a press conference. When he appeared at the Academy of Music in Philadelphia, he invited me to be the "reporter" coming onstage to question him as the Presidential candidate.

What a thrill that was for me. Duke Ellington's orchestra opened the show and Count Basie closed it. Slappy—and I—were the comedy relief right before intermission.

As we stood in the wings waiting to go on, the stage manager was on a phone talking to someone in the control booth at the back of the hall. He was directing the lighting according to one of Ellington's assistants. The assistant said, "Go to all blue lights." The stage manager repeated that into the phone and the stage became awash in blue. Then, the assistant said, "Now bring everything up for the closing." The guy on the phone reiterated that, and then all the lights came on.

Then, the stage manager turned to Slappy and asked, "Are you the next act?"

Slappy said, "Yeah."

The guy said, "How do you want your lights?"

Slappy calmly answered, "Make me look like a white man."

Without cracking a smile, the stage manager relayed into the phone, "Harry, this next act's a black act. I want you to make him look like a white man."

I was astounded when I walked onstage because the Academy of Music is a beautiful theatre with several rows of balconies ringing it. However, once I looked out from the stage, I couldn't see anything. The lights totally blinded me.

Then, as we began our act, I noticed a strange thing. The glare from the lights was white at first. Then it changed to white and yellow. Later, a blue light came on. Then, it switched to a red. In the middle of our routine, it dawned on me what was happening. The guy in the control booth must have been saying into the phone, "I don't know what the hell's going on. I've got the guy on the right looking like a white man, but I can't do anything with that guy on the left."

I began writing for Phyllis Diller through a friend at General Elec-

Phyllis Diller and I reviewing a few pages of new
jokes when she was appearing in New York City

tric, Ed Hercer. He worked a second job as a reporter for a local newspaper. One of his assignments was to interview Phyllis when she was
visiting the Philadelphia area. He mentioned that there was a guy
where he worked who wrote some pretty funny material. Phyllis said,
"Tell him to send me some. I'd like to see it."

I sent Phyllis two routines about Fang and her kids. She sent back
a check for $85. That was seventeen gags at $5 a gag. Phyllis bought
material from writers all over the country. In fact, once I was trying
to show some of my material to comedian, Jackie Vernon, who was
pretty hot at the time. When I introduced myself, I said, "I write a lot
of material for Phyllis Diller."

He said, "Who doesn't?"

I became part of an army of housewives across the nation, who wrote and sold gags to Phyllis. I got some notoriety for one of the early jokes Phyllis bought from me. That joke singled me out from the pack, I think.

In her act, Phyllis used to kid about her cooking. She did gags like: "I'm a terrible cook. I once went into my kitchen and caught a cockroach eating a Tum. I had a fire in my kitchen once. What happened was a grease fire broke out in my sink. The firemen put it out quickly, but 3 of them had to be treated for food inhalation."

I heard those routines and sent her a line that read: "I'll give you an idea how bad my cooking really is. Last Christmas the family chipped in and bought me an oven that flushes."

Years later when I was working on the Helen Reddy summer TV show, Joan Rivers walked by my office, popped her head in, and said, "I know you. You're the 'oven that flushes' guy."

Phyllis and I dealt mostly through the mail and occasionally over the phone. The first time I met Phyllis Diller was when she appeared at the Latin Casino in Philadelphia and invited me to see her performance. Six friends, my wife, and I went to see her one evening and the place was packed. As we stood in line, someone came out and called my name. When I responded, he said, "Phyllis would like to see you in her dressing room before the show."

My wife and I went backstage to meet her. The first thing she said to me was, "You're my best writer."

Rather than graciously accepting the compliment, I said, "Then how come I'm not in Hollywood?"

She said, "You're not ready yet."

It turned out to be the first of many lessons Phyllis taught me and it served me well throughout my career. It's better to be patient with career moves, rather than to rush into them before being prepared.

At that time, I was writing about thirty jokes a week for Phyllis. I didn't want to do more because I was afraid it would appear "pushy," and also I was afraid she'd balk at paying more.

She said, "Honey, I can afford to buy all the jokes you can give me. You've got to start writing more."

After that meeting I really started churning out one-liners for her act.

Of course, when we got back to our table, I told everyone about our meeting and how Phyllis had called me out of line. As we walked back to our car in the parking lot, I told them all about meeting Phyllis and how she had called me out of line outside the Latin Casino. As we drove home, I repeated the story of how I met Phyllis Diller after she had called me out of the line at the Latin Casino. Finally, someone shouted, "For God's sake, we heard the story already."

This was our table the night I first met Phyllis Diller in person.
My wife, Joanne, is third from the right. I'm second from the right—
the one laughing the hardest at my own jokes.

So, I shut up . . . for awhile. Then, I told them about it again, just in case, and maybe a few more times after that.

After Phyllis goaded me into writing more, I upped my weekly quota from thirty gags to sixty gags. For several weeks, I felt like the top of my head was going to explode, but eventually, I got used to the additional writing. Another lesson learned from Phyllis Diller—you can do more than you think you can.

When I sent material to Phyllis, she marked and numbered which gags she liked and sent me a check. Eventually, she called and said, "Look, I'm getting tired marking these jokes. About how much do I buy from you?"

I said, "It has averaged about $150 a week."

She said, "I'll send you a check for that amount each week and you just keep on writing jokes. OK?"

Of course, it was OK.

Each Friday, I took Phyllis' check to the bank and deposit it along with my salary. I gloried in the celebrity that check afforded. I pushed the checks toward the teller very casually, as if it was no big deal for me to be getting money from a nationally-known celebrity. I reveled in the double-take when the teller noticed the name on the check.

One time, the teller looked at the name and opened her eyes wide. She took that check to the teller at the next window, showed her the famous name, and they both chuckled.

When she came back to me, she said, "Phyllis Diller, huh?"

I said with all the false humility I could muster under the circumstances, "Yeah."

She said, "Is she anything like the real Phyllis Diller?"

Offended, I said, "That is the real Phyllis Diller."

The teller held the check up, examining it more closely, and said, "No, it's not."

Then she gave me my receipt and I left.

Chapter Five
The Break

Every successful career has a turning point, the "break." It's simply another link in the chain that's probably no more important than the hard work that preceded it, but it does mark a change of direction or intensity. Phyllis Diller provided my break when she starred in her own variety show on NBC in the 1968 television season. It was called *The Beautiful Phyllis Diller Show.*

Phyllis persuaded the producers of the show, Bernie Orenstein and Saul Turtletaub, that I should write her opening monologs. They had their agent, Bernie Weintraub, call me to arrange a deal. They were not prepared to hire me full-time, but they did want me to write material that Phyllis could use on the show.

Bernie Weintraub still laughs and tells the story of our first financial negotiations. He said, "How much do you make on your regular job?"

I asked, "With or without overtime?"

That got him chuckling on the phone. There was no overtime in Hollywood. Writers agreed to a price and worked as long as was necessary to get the job done. Bernie had never dealt with anyone who punched a time clock before.

I told him, "I make $12,000 a year, with overtime, $15,000."

He said, "We'll pay you $250 a week to work with Phyllis on the show."

I said, "Fine." It was fine because it more than doubled my income.

After we agreed to terms, though, I began to feel paranoid. I pictured those Hollywood producers grumbling about Phyllis Diller insisting on having some "non-pro" write her material. In my mind, they were cursing me for intruding into their producing arena. They were waiting, I thought, to get my first batch of jokes so they could take them to their star and say, "We're dumping this guy because he's incompetent, a mountebank, and an embarrassment to the comedy writing community."

Instead, they called the next day and congratulated me on my contract, welcomed me to the show's writing staff, and invited me to fly out and work with them for a week so I'd feel more comfortable about the show. "Would I be willing to do that?" they asked.

I told them, "First, I have to apologize to both of you."

"For what?" they asked.

"For all the terrible names I called you yesterday."

They sent me a first-class ticket—that's right, a first-class ticket—and $500 to cover incidental expenses along the way.

So much for my paranoia.

Of course, I was still a working man, so I had to arrange to visit Hollywood during my vacation. My wife and four children went to the seashore, where we usually spent our summer vacation, and I flew off to Tinseltown.

The producers welcomed me like a visiting dignitary. They introduced me to the staff writers and several producers on the NBC lot. They took me to dinner at elegant restaurants. To me, that was Big Time Show Business.

I was still a working man, used to traveling for the company. I kept a detailed account of all my expenses. At the end of the week, in saying goodbye to Bernie and Saul and thanking them for their gracious hospitality, I mentioned that I had money left over from the expense allowance they'd given me.

"How should we settle up?" I asked.

They said, "Take that money and fly to Las Vegas for the weekend."

They weren't interested in getting a formal expense account, nor did they want any of the money back.

Las Vegas was tempting, but I was more eager to get back and spend the weekend with my family at the seashore. They were expecting to meet me when they arrived back in Philadelphia on Monday, but instead, I wanted to surprise them by driving down and spending the weekend with them.

That's when I learned what the saying, "A prophet is never received in his own country," meant. I approached the house we had rented at the shore and peeked in the window. The kids were excited. They shouted, "Mommy, someone's looking in our window."

My wife turned, saw me, and said to them, "Oh, it's just your father."

I would have preferred, "Oh, it's probably some famous Hollywood writer," but all I got was, "It's just your father."

So much for my ego.

Working on a California-based show from Philadelphia was a challenge. I'd do monologue material and send it in advance. That was no real problem. However, the producers did like my material and wanted my input on the rest of the show. They sent me the completed script in the beginning of the week. There was no overnight mail or computer e-mail in those days, so I'd receive the script in the middle of the week.

I worked on the script through the night, adding jokes wherever I felt they improved the show. Then, I shaved, showered, and dropped the revised script into the mail on my way to work. One day a week, I went sleepless.

The producers appreciated my work, but the rest of the country apparently did not. The show drew low ratings and was cancelled in mid-season . . . along with my $250 stipend. It seemed I was right back where I started.

It was demoralizing, not only for me, but for my family. By then, I had been writing for about nine years. Although I made a little bit of money from my comedy, we did not spend any of it. Instead, we invested it with the idea that when the move to Hollywood happened, we'd have enough saved up to make it convenient.

However, it looked like no move to Hollywood was going to happen. So, my wife and I discussed my career and decided to abandon it. We were going to take the savings and buy a new house.

Fortunately, deciding on a house took time. Before we found anything we wanted to spend our life savings on, I got another call from Bernie Weintraub. Since the cancellation of Phyllis Diller's show, he had been scouting up work for me in television.

Orenstein and Turtletaub were hired to do *That Girl,* the situation comedy starring Marlo Thomas. They knew I wasn't ready for situation comedy writing yet, but they did feel I could work as a staff writer on a variety show. They mentioned my name and recommended my work to several other producers who would be working in variety, and they convinced their agent, Weintraub, that he could place me on some staff.

He had two potential shows—one featuring Jimmy Durante and the Lennon Sisters, and the other a variety show featuring Jim Nabors, who became a bankable television star with his hit sitcom, *Gomer Pyle*.

Bernie told me, "Write some samples of what you would do for both shows and get them to me."

I did, and the Jim Nabors producers made the first offer.

I took it.

I was going to Hollywood.

I was delighted, but not everyone was. When I told my mom that I was leaving General Electric to become a television writer, she said, "What? And give up all that security?"

The "break" not only altered the direction of my career, but I discovered it also changed the way people thought about me.

General Electric was predictably very supportive. When I informed my superiors there, they all said, "Should you come back, your job will be waiting for you." That was a tremendous offer because it took some of the fear out of the adventure. If Hollywood rejected me, we would've spent the money that we had put aside for that purpose and returned to the same job I left. All it would've cost would've been my loss of seniority and a week or two of vacation time.

Others weren't so encouraging. At a goodbye party some friends threw for my wife and I, one of those friends commented on my hair. It was slightly long because I needed a haircut. He said, "Getting a little artsy, aren't we?"

I made a mental note never to send him any autographed copies of any books I wrote in the future.

The funniest put down I received, though, was from a person at General Electric that I didn't even know. She went to Ed Hercer, the editor of the plant newspaper, who happened to be one of my closest friends, and she gave him the scoop.

"There's a person who works over in Medium Voltage who has been writing jokes for Carol Burnett and now he's going to Hollywood."

Ed corrected her. "He's actually been writing for Phyllis Diller."

She insisted, "No, he writes for Carol Burnett. His name is Gene Perret." She pronounced my name with the accent on the last syllable, just like Carol Burnett.

Hercer knew I pronounced my name "Perret" with the accent on the first syllable to rhyme with that little animal, the ferret. He corrected her, pronouncing my name correctly.

She said, "No, it's Perret." She still made it sound like Burnett.

It was useless to argue, so Ed said, "Fine, we will run a story about him in the company paper."

The following day, that lady came back to the newspaper office and said to Ed Hercer, "You know that guy I was telling you about? Gene Perret?" She pronounced it incorrectly again.

He said, "Yeah?"

She said, "Well, he's getting so uppity now that he changed his name to 'Perret.'" She pronounced it the way I've been pronouncing it since birth.

I didn't care. I was going to Hollywood.

Chapter Six
Television Writing Protocol

Yes, I was going to Hollywood, but I had no idea what to expect once I got there. I had studied comedy writing and served about a nine-year apprenticeship writing material for standup comedians. As one producer said about my work, "You certainly know your way around a joke." Sure, I could sit at my kitchen table back in Philadelphia and write gags about whatever topics were current, send them off, and get a check occasionally. That's what I knew about comedy writing.

About television comedy writing, I knew very little. I had more questions than answers. What was I expected to write about? How long would I have to write it? Would I be writing alone or with a partner? Maybe I'd be writing with a whole roomful of other comedy writers? Who would be deciding whether my writing was acceptable or not?

Many people wonder how television shows get written. Some of the questions I'm frequently asked are: "How many writers are on a show?" "Is your writing life anything like the old *Dick Van Dyke Show*?"

Everything that goes on in front of the cameras is seen by most of the nation. People accept that Lucy Ricardo will cause some sort of trouble and that Ricky Ricardo will be furious, frustrated, and finally forgiving. Folks know where Edith and Archie Bunker live and how they're likely to behave. They're familiar with Joey, Phoebe, Monica, Chandler, Ross and Rachel—the gang from *Friends*. They feel as though they should be able to barge unannounced into Seinfeld's apartment just the way Kramer did. If they sat at the bar in *Cheers*, they'd begin to trade one-liners with all the regulars.

Since the writing of the television shows is done behind the camera, though, it remains a mystery to most of us. It certainly was a mystery to me, as I headed towards Hollywood.

Permit me, then, to flash forward to a point well into my television writing career. I knew a little bit more about the protocol of writing a television show at that point. So, it might be a good idea to discuss some of the procedures involved in writing for a television show.

Most of my writing fell into three main categories: weekly variety shows, situation comedies, and specials. Let's look into each of them separately.

Weekly Variety Shows:

Production on a typical weekly variety show usually followed a five-day schedule. Most of the shows I wrote for ran from Monday to Friday. Although the scripts are written in advance, the actual production work began with the table reading on Monday morning. A table reading was where the cast sat around a table, scripts in hand, and read through the entire teleplay. Each of the writers took notes along the way, marking jokes that didn't work, or might be dropped or replaced, and any spots where the story line seemed awkward, or the pace of the comedy slowed down. In short, we marked up our copies of the script where we felt the show could be improved.

The performers also voiced any reservations they had about the script. Some questioned the motivation or asked for funnier dialogue. Others requested an explanation from the writers or producers for certain moments in the script.

That first reading of the script was an opportunity for the cast, the creative staff, and the stage crew to spot potential deficiencies.

After the table reading, the cast and the director went into the rehearsal hall to get the show "on its feet." That's a phrase we used that meant to transform the teleplay from just words on paper to active performing by the cast. The writers generally weren't invited to these rehearsals. First, we all had work to do to prepare for upcoming shows, and second, it was less inhibiting for the performers to add physical moves and suggest line changes without the writers present.

Of course, if there was a problem that needed clarification, or a segment of the show that demanded immediate creative attention, they called in the writers to see and hear the problem and help to resolve it.

The writers, after the table reading, met with the producers to discuss their notes. If rewrites were required after that get-together, certain writers were assigned that task. Those who had no rewrites for the current show continued to work on material for upcoming shows.

On Wednesday afternoon, after the cast had two days of rehearsal, they, along with the creative staff and the stage crew gathered for a run-through. The run-through was a performance in a rehearsal hall of the entire show. There were no stage costumes involved and only minimal props. The sets were indicated by taped lines on the floor. However, the run-through gave the technical people a chance to see what was expected for the actual taping. It gave the performers a feel for how the show would be received by a live audience, and, of course, the writers could also visualize where some changes might be made.

After the run-through, the performers and writers met with the producers to exchange notes and decide on rewrites. The writers then met as a group to make the changes quickly so that new scripts could be delivered to the cast that evening and they could be prepared for the next morning's rehearsal. Wednesday, for the writing staff, usually meant rewriting sessions that lasted until late in the evening or even early into the morning.

All day Thursday and Friday, the cast and crew had rehearsals on stage. At those sessions, camera angles were figured out, movements on stage were planned, and so on. Again, unless there were specific problems that required immediate attention, the writers weren't involved. We were busy writing for upcoming show episodes.

On Friday afternoon, we had a "Dress Rehearsal." It was called a rehearsal, but it was actually a full taping of the show complete with a live audience. The writers usually watched that show on a television monitor in the producer's office. We took notes on areas of the show that we felt could be improved.

After the dress rehearsal, the cast, producers, and writers met and quickly decided on any changes that might be made on the spot, and those were delivered to the cast in the form of notes. They studied these changes and incorporated them into the next taping of the show—the final air taping, which was done almost immediately following that meeting.

In effect, we had two complete versions of the show on tape and the director and producers later decided, in editing, how to intercut the best versions of each performance into the finished tape that was delivered to the network for broadcast.

On one episode of *The Carol Burnett Show,* characters played by Carol Burnett and Harvey Korman were having a romantic dinner. The crew lit the candles on the table for one show, but forgot to light them for the other taping. When the show aired, the viewers watched the candles go out and then magically re-light themselves during the sketch.

The writing for those shows, of course, had to be done in advance. The writers spent most of their time working on sketches and bits of comedy that were used on shows that might be three, four, or five weeks later in the schedule.

Writing on a variety show took many different forms. The writing staff brainstormed as a group in order to come up with workable ideas for a given show or a given guest star. At the brainstorming sessions, we threw out possible ideas, discussed them, changed them around, and then had the head-writer either reject the premise or give the go-ahead. Along with the go-ahead, one team of writers was assigned that particular sketch idea to develop into a fully-written comedy piece.

To give you an idea of how the process worked, at one session, a writer talked about dining out the evening before. He and his girl-friend went out to dinner and their waitress had another girl following her around the entire time. The second girl never spoke. Finally, they asked what the reason for this was. The waitress explained that she was a new girl, who was in training. She was learning to become a waitress.

The group liked the craziness of that idea, but couldn't immediately figure out how to use it in a comedy sketch. Then two writers announced that they wanted to give it a try.

The resulting sketch worked very well on the show. Carol Burnett was a bank teller in the sketch. Harvey Korman came in, handed her a note, brandished a weapon, and demanded money. He was about to rob the bank. Carol called over Vicki Lawrence. She explained that Vicki was a "teller in training" and she should be involved. Harvey Korman then signaled for Tim Conway, who entered the scene. Harvey explained that he was teaching Tim how to be a bank robber. At the end of the sketch, a policeman came in and, of course, called for another policeman, who was really a "policeman in training."

Most of the writing on variety shows was done by teams of two writers. It sometimes took from two days to a week to finish a first draft of a comedy sketch. The head-writer then reviewed the sketch, made notes, and handed it back to the original writing team for changes. Sometimes a sketch was discussed and rewritten by the entire writing team. The completed sketch was handed in to the producers and could have been rejected, but usually was slotted into one of the upcoming shows.

Situation Comedies:

Situation comedies were those shows that had a story each week as opposed to variety shows that were composed of unrelated musical numbers, comedy bits, and guest star performances.

The production schedule on situation comedies was pretty much the same as the variety shows. They began with the table reading. Then, the cast rehearsed, taped the show, and then the process started over again for the following week's show. However, the writing protocol was slightly different.

Many situation comedies were written on a freelance basis. Writers sold the show one episode at a time. The process began with the pitch session. That was where a team of writers were invited into the producers' offices to present story ideas. Then, the producers either rejected the ideas or bought one.

If the writers made a sale, they were usually invited to turn in an outline. From that, the producers took notes, usually scheduled another meeting, and handed the writers suggested rewrites.

The writers then wrote the script for the entire episode.

The original writers then were generally out of the loop. Any rewrites required after that were handled by the in-house writing staff.

The in-house writing staff was writers working permanently on the specific sitcom. They occasionally wrote episodes for the show, but in that capacity, they functioned and were paid as freelance contributors. However, their main function on the show was comparable to staff writers on a variety show. They attended rehearsals, took notes, offered suggestions, and did those rewrites that were required after the freelance writers were no longer involved.

Specials:

Specials were . . . special. Each one was handled however the producers wanted to handle them. The writing took any form that fit the producers' concept. Because of that, it was hard to define any single procedure.

That's a brief analysis of what television comedy writing entailed. Of course, as I mentioned, I knew none of that on the day I arrived in Hollywood.

Chapter Seven
Engineer in Hollywood

The day I arrived in California, I sent Phyllis Diller a telegram: "Have been in Hollywood for two hours. Not yet a star. Please advise."

This was a strange world to me, and I must have seemed even stranger to it. Hollywood was a place for beautiful and talented people with lofty aspirations. I was an engineer falling through the looking glass into Wonderland. On my first day at work, I wore a white shirt and tie. The other writers did not wear white shirts and ties; they did not even own white shirts and ties.

Years later, when I was on *The Carol Burnett Show* staff, another writer was going to be married. He borrowed a suit, tie, and shirt from the wardrobe department for his Saturday nuptials, and then he returned the strange apparel when he returned to work.

More offensive than the shirt and tie, though, was the pocket protector that I wore—the kind that nerds wore. The mechanical pencils that I carried in it were arranged by colors. The black pencil that we engineers used for our drafting work was to the left. To the right of that was the red pencil that signified a deletion on our electrical drawings. To the right of that was the yellow pencil that we used for marking additions.

The shirt, tie, and strategically organized pocket protector went after the first day at the writing offices. I can take a joke as well as anybody, but I could not endure 743 of them a day.

Even out of uniform, I was still an engineer. The producers had me share an office with a more experienced writer. I asked him, "When do we go to lunch?"

He said, "Whenever."

I asked, "How long do we get for lunch?"

He said, "As long as you want."

I looked confused and almost offended by that freedom. I wanted supervision, someone to guide my actions.

He noticed and said to me, "Schmuck, you're a big shot now. Start acting like one."

It wasn't easy for me. Though I bought new clothes—what I thought would be more appropriate clothes—my fellow writers still kidded me about my dress. One day after lunch, I noted on my desk calendar how much I paid for lunch. *Such records might be useful,* I thought, *in submitting my tax deductions.*

One of the other writers noticed the figure $8.95 on my desk calendar. He said, "What'd you do, buy a new suit?"

I didn't mind the kidding so much, but I did feel uneasy at work. Everyone was kind, generous, and supportive, but I didn't feel at home yet. For many years, I did all my writing at the kitchen table. I was going to make my official logo a gravy stain. My writing was solitary, lonely, but then it moved into a busy office with veteran writers. Everything I wrote was scrutinized, discussed at meetings, and rewritten. It became hard for me to write. My fingers froze over the keyboard.

My solution was to fake it. I showed up at the office, but did very little creative, original work there. In the evening after dinner, I did all my writing lying across my bed in the motel room, which was my headquarters until I found a permanent home in Southern California.

There, I was alone, away from the wisecracks and the instant critiques. I concentrated on my work. The jokes simmered in my brain for awhile before they were committed to paper.

Then, the next morning, I took all my notes and jokes to the CBS offices and typed them out, pretending that I was creating on the spot.

It worked, at least until I became more comfortable with my surroundings and my colleagues. I thought I was a good comedy writer, but I just had to get used to being part of a comedy writing staff.

Those first several weeks were difficult and frightening. My contract ran for only thirteen shows. After that, if they didn't pick up my option, I was to be unemployed and on a whole different coast from where I could get employment. However, the discomfort I felt and the hardships I endured were all worth it. I was a comedy writer for television. No one could destroy the thrill of that, but one guy came close.

My family did not make the trip to the west coast with me. My wife and four kids remained behind to finish the school year; they wouldn't join me for several weeks. So, as I mentioned, I booked a room in a motel across the street from CBS Television City. I did my shopping in a supermarket a few doors further down the block.

A gentleman seemed to be following me. I saw him on the street and in the supermarket. He seemed very interested in me. What frightened me was that he was not very neat or clean-looking. He had long hair, a scraggly beard, and terrible-looking clothing. I thought he was a homeless person.

He probably thinks that I'm a celebrity, I thought. In my mind's eye, I was because I was writing for television. *How much more of a celebrity can one be? He probably also knows I'm rich.* Again, in my mind's eye, I was. My salary was more than I ever dreamed of, and I could not see how the stars were making much more than I, nor could I believe that they were. *What on earth would they spend it on?* I felt he was either going to rob me or kidnap me for a healthy ransom.

Then, one day in the supermarket, he made his move. He came to me and said, "You write for television, don't you?"

I started backing away from him, but said, "Yes, I do."

He came closer, making up the ground that I had gained in backing off, and said, "You work on one of the shows across the street, don't you?"

I said, "Yes."

He said, "So do I. I'm writing on Glen Campbell's show."

I did not know whether to feel good at that news or not. I was happy that he was not going to do me any harm, but I was unhappy that such a bizarre-looking creature was in the same profession I was. I was happy that I was working in television and on a show that the experts were predicting would be the runaway hit of the new shows for the upcoming season—*The Jim Nabors Hour.*

Chapter Eight
The Jim Nabors Hour

Being at the famous CBS studios, entering the building each morning through the "Artist Entrance," passing celebrities in the corridors, writing on a national television show, and working with veterans who had written for legends like Jack Benny and George Burns was overwhelming to me. The writers' meetings were especially intimidating. I was hesitant to speak up.

Often, we discussed a problem with the script and I'd have an idea, but was reluctant to verbalize it. Those guys picked on me enough for my clothes; I didn't want my ideas ridiculed, too.

The meeting continued with many suggestions offered and rejected. Then, someone came up with the very idea that I had been keeping locked securely in my private world. They said something like, "Why don't we let Jim Nabors play the dummy role and have Frank Sutton play the ventriloquist?" Everyone in the room shouted huzzahs. "That's a great idea. Reverse the roles. Wonderful idea! Brilliant idea!"

I wanted to stand and shout, "I thought of that twenty minutes ago, but I was too shy to tell you guys." It was too late for that, though. All I could do was vow that next time I would speak up sooner, but I didn't for a long time.

Those first few months were difficult for me, a first time staff writer. My cockiness kept me going, though. I knew I was funny and a superb writer. I believed that firmly until I wrote something.

After I handed in my first complete sketch, the producers, Duke Vincent and Bruce Johnson, called me into their office. I went expecting glorious kudos and a generous raise.

"This sketch needs a major rewrite," is what I got.

I said, "Really? I think that sketch is very funny."

"But it needs work," Duke and Bruce insisted.

I said, "I don't think I can make it much funnier than that. I worked hard on it and don't think it needs a big rewrite."

The producers were patient with me and very kind. They said, "Do you really think it's funny?"

I said, "Yes."

They asked, "Do you think it's perfect as is?"

I said, "I think it is."

They said, "Fine, then let's read it through."

"All right," I agreed. I was sure that once they heard this out loud they would see the error of their initial judgment.

They each took certain parts to read and assigned me the role of the star. I was to read the Jim Nabors part.

We began.

The first joke got a nice laugh from them.

"That's a good joke," Duke said.

I accepted the compliment quietly and modestly because I knew it was a very good joke.

We read some more and the script drew several more good laughs.

Then we read and we read and we read.

They stopped, and Bruce asked, "Have you noticed anything?"

I said, "Yes."

Duke said, "What?"

I said, "I haven't said anything for a very long time."

Bruce said, "You haven't spoken for twelve pages."

Duke said, "Your sketch is very funny, but you have the star of the show standing on stage 'catching flies.'"

I then knew the sketch badly needed a major rewrite, so I gathered up the pages and went back to my office.

I learned a lot on that writing staff. Among other things, I learned that the other writers were nuts. One time, I had lunch with my writing partner at the famous Joe Allen's restaurant. As we were leaving, a tourist couple stopped us at the front door and said to my partner, "Sir, would you take a picture of my wife and me in front of this restaurant?"

Without missing a beat or a step, he said to them, "I would love to, but I don't have my camera with me," and continued walking.

The gentleman stared after him with a look of bewilderment on his face and, of course, his own instamatic in his hand.

The writers continued to kid me as the naïve newcomer to the profession, but they also welcomed me to the fraternity. They allowed me to become a part of their drinking group that met almost daily at the City Slicker, a bar across the street from the CBS Television City Studios, and they arranged for me to open up a running bar tab there.

It was very helpful because the home I rented, when I wearied of motel living after about a week, was a good freeway ride away from Hollywood. We quit work around six o'clock most evenings. If I tried to journey home during that rush hour traffic, it took me over an hour. However, if I went across to the City Slicker and sat there having a few drinks until eleven o'clock, there was hardly any traffic at all.

The City Slicker was a gathering spot for many show business people working at CBS. My wife stayed home with the children when I first came to Hollywood. They finished the school year and then unloaded our home back east, but the family didn't join me until about a month after my arrival.

When my wife got to town, I took her in to meet my fellow workers. We stopped at the City Slicker. The waitress came to our table and said to me, "The usual, Gene?"

My wife noticed and kidded me about it. She said, "I see. I've been home struggling with the kids and the sale of the house and you've been out here getting yourself drunk, huh?"

The waitress didn't realize my wife was joking, and she tried to save me. She said to my spouse, "No. As much as I've seen Gene drink, I've never seen him drunk."

Being a writer, I felt she could have phrased that a little differently. Maybe lose the phrase, "As much as I've seen Gene drink."

Somehow, my fellow writers, the producers, and my wife allowed me to survive the pre-production period. That's the time when we worked on the show, but we didn't actually produce any shows. The staff developed ideas and scripts to be ready for when the stars arrived and we went into production. That would be when we started putting the show on tape and over the airwaves.

However, the first week of production almost ended my brief television writing career. During the first run-through rehearsal of

The cast of *The Jim Nabors Hour.* Pictured l. to r. – Karen Morrow, Frank Sutton, Jim Nabors, Ronnie Schell.

the show, we almost lost our star. We had a regular, weekly sketch on the show in which Frank Sutton played Jim Nabors's brother-in-law. They ran a boarding house together. In the sketch, Frank invariably got upset with Jim over some plot twist or another. At that first rehearsal, he was to get so angry at the Nabors character that he threatened him with a fireplace poker. Since that was only a rehearsal, the prop guys got some old poker from somewhere. While Frank Sutton was brandishing the weapon, the pointed head of it flew off and went straight up in the air, came down, and embedded itself into the hardwood floor right next to the star of our show.

Six inches to the left, and I would have retrieved my pocket protector and been out looking for an electrical engineering job.

Run-throughs were sometimes exciting because the celebs were there, but there was no pressure. The cameras weren't on, and the audience wasn't present. It was simply a rehearsal for the cast, staff, and crew. The guest stars, who wanted to be crazy, could be.

We had a short talk spot written for guest, Don Rickles, and Jim Nabors. In the script, it ran less than three minutes. At the run-through, Don, with his string of adlibs, kept it going for over twenty minutes, and we laughed practically the entire time.

At one point, when there was a brief lull in the laughter, Don turned to Jim Nabors and said, "You sing beautifully? Are you sure you're not Gordon MacCrea's long lost illegitimate son." It got big laughs. Everything Rickles said at that rehearsal got big laughs.

The producers had to end that thing so we could move on to our writers meeting and get a revised script ready for shooting. They signaled Frank Sutton to interrupt Don's soliloquy with his scripted entrance.

Frank obediently walked on, but it didn't stop Rickles. He looked at Sutton and said, "What the hell are you doing out here? If I grab your legs, you'll turn into a waffle."

Of course, that brought howls of laughter from all of us at the rehearsal.

Don Rickles said, "What are you people laughing at? That didn't even make any sense to me."

At another run-through, we were rehearsing a circus finale, a big musical number that featured the entire cast. At one point, Karen Morrow, one of the co-stars of the show, was to ride an elephant. Since we used minimal props at the run-through, the prop guys got some sort of life-sized papier-mâché elephant on wheels. Unfortunately, it wasn't very stable.

Karen rode the fake pachyderm for just a few beats before she and the elephant tumbled over. For Karen it was a fall from a considerable height, so everyone got up from their chairs and rushed to her aid. She wasn't seriously hurt, but certainly shaken up a bit.

Then, we had to decide whether to continue with the rehearsal or end it there because of the mishap. One of the writers chipped in with, "I'd continue. If she doesn't get right back up there, she'll never ride a fake elephant again."

The writers' meeting following those rehearsals was sometimes as bizarre as the rehearsal itself. We once wrote a sketch for Jim Nabors and guest star, Tennessee Ernie Ford. It was a takeoff on a hit show at that time, *Ironside*. That show was about a detective confined to a wheelchair. Of course, ours was a hick version of that show, so instead of sitting in a wheelchair, Ernie Ford sat in a wheelbarrow and had Jim Nabors, as his assistant, wheel him around.

The sketch died at the rehearsal. It needed drastic revisions, so at the writers' meeting immediately following the run-through, we concentrated on fixing or replacing our sketch, called "Ironbottom."

Some wanted to replace it with another sketch that was scheduled for later in the season. Other writers felt that we could give it a late-night rework and have a viable sketch ready for the next morning.

One writer, Al Gordon, thought the sketch was alright as it was with one minor exception. He said, "Lose the wheelbarrow and get a live donkey."

None of us agreed with that fix, but he persisted.

Eventually Al said, "Look, get a live donkey. If the donkey urinates onstage, you've got a hit sketch."

Another very funny writer, Arnie Kogen, said, "Yeah, or even if Ernie does."

We revised the sketch, leaving the wheelbarrow in, and it still got few laughs. Apparently, we were funnier at the meeting than we were at the typewriter.

Al Gordon, a long-time Jack Benny writer with his partner, Hal Goldman, was famous for contradictory statements, often within the same sentence. One time, all the Nabors writers were feeling paranoid. We were complaining about something or another that happened in the offices.

Al cheered us up by reminding us that writers on every show throughout the history of television complained. It was commonplace. "Except," he corrected himself, "on *The Jack Benny Show*."

He said, "Hal and I worked for twenty-five years on that show. We shared an office with two other writers and we never had a problem. There was never a complaint, never any backstabbing. For twenty-five years, we worked together with no problems at all."

Then he added, "Except that Hal and I knew that we were doing all the work."

Al Gordon came into the writing offices one morning after having attended a Writers Guild meeting the night before. At the meeting, there was talk of a strike and feelings were running pretty high.

Those of us who didn't attend the meeting had heard about a writer, who got up to speak at the microphone the strike committee had positioned at the front of the aisle so that each member's questions and comments could be heard. That particular writer collapsed at the microphone and was taken from the hall.

Since Al was at the meeting, we asked about the incident. Al Gordon told us, "It was terrible. I was sitting right next to the microphone, you know. This guy got up to speak and in the middle of his question he fell over, right at my feet. I got up and ran away."

Then he added with disdain, "Do you think any of those other writers would come to help him?"

I learned a lot that first year on writing staff. I learned, for instance, that the creative people in Hollywood don't give normal Christmas gifts. Arnie Kogen spent one day calling banks to see if he could buy a series of Polish war bonds as gifts for several of his business associates. One of the bank executives told him quite vigorously that he should be ashamed of himself for contributing to Poland's economy. She said, "Don't you know they're at war with us?"

Arnie abandoned that shopping spree, not because of her admonition, but because he couldn't find any place that sold Polish war bonds. So, for each of his friends, all of whom lived in the pleasant climate of Southern California, Arnie purchased and gift-wrapped one snow tire.

We writers had a picture taken of ourselves surrounding the large logo that we used to open the show each week. That was our Christmas present to Jim Nabors. Jim enjoyed it and hung it over the couch in his office.

The following year, though, the joke sort of backfired. We all went over to NBC and had our picture taken with Flip Wilson. Flip's new show was on opposite the Jim Nabors Hour. It seemed funny at the time, but by the end of the year, Flip had outdrawn us in the ratings, and *The Jim Nabors Hour* was cancelled.

I wonder where those photos are today.

Another thing that I learned during my rookie year in Hollywood was that I was not the big shot that I thought I was.

My wife convinced me that I should invite some neighbors to see a taping of the Nabors show. So, I arranged for VIP tickets—no waiting in line outside the studio. By giving my name to the page on duty, my guests were escorted into the studio and given preferred seats.

After the taping, the writers had to meet for changes and rewrites to get ready for the next taping, so I couldn't join those folks for dinner. I did, though, arrange, with my new pre-approved credit, for them to have cocktails and dinner on me at the City Slicker.

The next morning was Saturday, and that gentleman noticed me sitting in my back yard, so he came down the street to join me. I presumed he wanted to thank me for an entertaining and exciting evening. I presumed wrong.

He pulled up a chair, got comfortable in my back yard, and the first words out of his mouth were, "You know what's wrong with that show?"

Chapter Nine
Bob Hope Calls

Around 1959, I first decided that I might try comedy writing as a livelihood. I figured I should learn a little bit about the craft. Bob Hope's material seemed to be the best to study. It was good performance comedy, but it also translated well to the written word. Even though Hope's expert timing and delivery helped each gag, the material was still funny when you read quotes of it in the paper. Other comics could be hilarious, but much of their effectiveness depended on their stage antics. Jerry Lewis, for instance, was not very quotable.

So I decided to study Bob Hope. He and his writers became my mentors. I made an audio tape of each one of Bob Hope's opening monologues from his television specials. I typed out the material and studied it to learn the form of gags he used, their sequences, and how he worded the jokes. I became very familiar with Hope's rapid-fire style of one-line comedy.

Then, I put the monologue away for a while. After a few weeks, I picked several current topics from the newspapers and tried to write new material on those topical items using the format and style that was in the Bob Hope monologue. That was my homemade course in comedy writing.

Flash forward to one weekend late in March 1970. I had just finished doing some yard work. After a shower, I planned to simply relax for the remainder of the weekend, preparing for another tough week of work on the Nabors show. While I was in the shower, my wife answered the phone.

"Gene," she hollered, "It's for you."

Interrupting my musical numbers in the shower irritated me. I shouted loudly, "Find out who it is and tell them I'll call back." My melodious vocal continued.

She hollered again, "It's Bob Hope."

I zoomed past her and picked up the phone. I didn't towel off, I didn't even grab a towel. I stood dripping wet, naked, in the kitchen talking to my idol and mentor.

"Hello," I adlibbed.

"Gene?" Bob Hope said.

"Yes," I further quipped.

"This is Bob Hope."

And it was. It sounded as though I was listening to one of my taped monologues from my comedy writing formative years.

"Right," I said. I was, in effect, telling Bob Hope that he knew who he was.

He said, "I've heard that you write some pretty funny stuff."

"I do," I said.

"How'd you like to write some stuff for me?"

"I'd love to," I said.

"Listen, I'm emceeing the Academy Awards next week and I could use a few jokes. Could you write some and get them to me in a hurry?"

"Sure," I said. "Is tomorrow OK?"

He said, "Yeah, or Monday's all right."

"OK," I said.

Click . . . dial tone.

I was so excited. I told my wife the good news.

"I'm going to get some paper and sit out back and start working on this right away."

My wife said, "Maybe you ought to put some clothes on first and then mop up the mess you made on the kitchen floor."

I did and I did, and then I sat in my special writing place in the back yard and wrote out 130 jokes in longhand on a yellow legal pad. I arranged them into a routine and typed them later.

John Wayne was nominated for an Academy Award that year for his portrayal of Rooster Cogburn in *True Grit*. So, I had Bob Hope walk onstage wearing an eye patch and I wrote several jokes off that. One was: "You were right, John. This does go well with a pot belly."

He didn't do that one.

Another one was: "I just wear this when I watch reruns of my road pictures." Then, pointing to the patch, he added, "This eye is for Crosby."

He didn't do that one, either.

He opened with a variation of one of my suggestions. Wearing the patch when he walked onstage, he said, "You remember me . . . Moshe."

That, of course, was a reference to Moshe Dayan, a famous Israeli General, who wore an eye patch before John Wayne did.

Another nominated film that year was *The Sterile Cuckoo*. In my material, I had Bob Hope say, "I went to see *The Sterile Cuckoo*. I thought it was the life of Tiny Tim."

Hope did that one.

He did ten of my lines in his opening monologue that night. Since he only did thirty lines in the entire monologue, I felt that, for a beginner, I had a pretty good percentage.

Hope agreed. The next morning, he called me and said, "I liked your stuff. It looks like you've been writing for me all your life."

I said, "I have, Mr. Hope, only you didn't know about it."

We agreed to a writing arrangement there on the phone and I wrote for Bob Hope from then until he retired from performing in 1997.

I did check with the Nabors producers. No sense ruining a career at the outset by doing something unethical. They gave me permission to write for Hope, but asked that I refrain from taking screen credit because the Hope show often aired opposite the Nabors show. That was all right with me. I was still writing for Bob Hope.

Circumstances almost destroyed that gig for me, though. I had told Phyllis Diller about Hope's phone call and she was delighted. She also idolized Bob Hope and considered him a mentor. She said to me, "Honey, if there's any material you've given me that you want to give to Bob, go right ahead. It's perfectly all right with me."

There were a few lines that I had written for Phyllis's act that could be used at the Academy Awards. In fact, the *Sterile Cuckoo* line was first written for Phyllis. I sent it to Bob, and there were a few others.

The problem was that Phyllis was to co-host a pre-Oscar show. In Los Angeles, it aired several days before the Academy Awards telecast. Of course, I watched the show. Phyllis did many of the lines that I had sent to Bob Hope.

I panicked.

That show was scheduled to air in most other cities immediately before the Academy Awards show. That meant that Phyllis would be seen doing a line on national television, and minutes later, Bob would be seen onstage at the Oscar show doing the same line. Someone would surely notice. Someone would surely comment. Someone would surely get fired—perhaps by both Phyllis and Bob.

I tried to reach Bob, but couldn't. He was busy preparing for his emceeing chores. On the day of the Oscar telecast, my family was enjoying an outing to Disneyland. I wasn't. I was there, but I wasn't really enjoying it.

I had to reach Bob before he went onstage.

Every time we passed a public phone at Disneyland, I called Bob's house. "He can't be disturbed right now," the secretary would say. "Can I have him call you back?"

"No, I can't be reached. I'll try again."

I called again, but couldn't get through.

I called again, and again, and again. All the while, I was getting more and more depressed because I fantasized a major scandal about two comedians doing the same joke. Hollywood would blacklist me. The writing community would disown me. The Writer's Guild of America would burn my membership card.

Finally, I got through. I explained to Bob, "I wrote for Phyllis and she invited me, gave me permission, said it was OK, told me there'd be no problem if I sent a few of the jokes I'd given her to you." Then,

I told him about the television show she did and that she did some of the jokes that I sent to him. I was prepared to be scolded and perhaps punished. It was fitting and proper that I should be. I fully expected never to write for Bob again.

Calmly, Hope said, "*Which jokes?*"

I read him a list of them and he said, "OK, I'll take them out. Thanks for calling."

He understood and handled the situation like a true gentleman. He was a gentleman for all the years I worked for him.

Chapter Ten
Laugh-In

My God, it was all over.

For the previous two years, I had worked on a successful television variety show, made good money, met some famous movie stars, and worked with talented, creative, fun people. Then, it was all gone.

That's the way I felt when I heard that *The Jim Nabors Hour* was cancelled and would not be renewed for the coming season.

The Jim Nabors Hour got off to a roaring start. Even before the show aired, it was picked to be the solid hit for the 1969-1970 season by some advertising people, who supposedly knew things like that in advance. They were right. The first show aired on September 25, 1969, and got mixed reviews but spectacular numbers in the ratings. We finished #4 for that season. CBS loved us and they loved Jim Nabors.

The second year, we were opposite a new variety show on NBC, *The Flip Wilson Show*. Flip did well and knocked us down a few notches in the Nielsen ratings, but it wasn't really Flip's success that caused the cancellation. Our show was still doing well in the ratings. We were no longer #4 in the nation, but we weren't much below that. We were still ranked higher than *The Carol Burnett Show,* yet her show was renewed.

CBS was embarrassed by their reputation as a "hayseed" network. Some other shows that CBS cancelled during the 1970-1971 season were *Mayberry RFD, The Beverly Hillbillies, Green Acres,* and *Hee Haw.* Jim Nabors was considered a little too "hayseed" to stay on the network, although Glen Campbell's *Goodtime Hour* survived another season.

Although I was a relative rookie in the television world, I sensed that it could be a cruel atmosphere. When you're up, you're up; when you're down, you're a lot more than down. You become a pariah, a leper, good for nothing but the set up for various put-down gags.

Being out of work in the writing profession was scary, because I never knew if I was ever going back to work again. It was also exhilarating. While I worked, I was out of circulation. I had a job and an income. When I was out of work, though, I was available. People wanted me.

If terminated from engineering, a worker had to go looking for work. In show business, work came looking me, so it was a rather heady sensation.

Then, too, there was the thrill of negotiating, and I could be quite bold in my negotiations because I didn't do it face to face. I had an agent who acted as my "muscle." Agents are good at that.

That reminds me of Bob Hope's joke about Ronald Reagan when he first ran for President. Bob said, "Reagan is one politician who doesn't lie, cheat, or steal. He has an agent who does that for him." It's uncomfortably close to true.

Let me tell you a story about typical agent "muscle." A writer friend of mine had a birthday party at his house. It was on a very interesting night for those in Los Angeles. A few weeks earlier, Notre

Dame's basketball team had defeated UCLA and ended their record streak of unbeaten games at 88. That particular night was the rematch. UCLA was out for revenge, and most sports fans wanted to watch it.

When we arrived at the house, that writer's wife told us that no one was to touch the television set because it was a birthday celebration. No stupid basketball game was going to take center stage. All of us at the party obeyed meekly.

A bit later, my agent arrived. He burst through the door and shouted, "What the hell's going on here? The ball game's on." With that, he marched over to the television set, turned the game on, and sat down and watched it. We huddled around behind him and watched, too.

That's the kind of chutzpah that agents lent to the writers they represented. We wouldn't dare ask for certain things, but we had no hesitation about telling our agent what we "demanded." We had him or her ask for it, and they did.

So, there's a certain sense of power in tangling with major players like NBC, CBS, ABC, or production company executives over what we wanted or what we'd settle for . . . provided that it was our agent who went in and was forceful in our place.

So, it was kind of a nice feeling when my agent called and said, "*Laugh-In* wants you." *Laugh-In* was a landmark show in television comedy. It was a smash when it premiered in 1968, and it was still going strong.

They wanted me, and I was thrilled. I was thrilled, that is, until I found out how much they wanted me for. They offered less than I was making per show on my second year on *The Jim Nabors Hour.* Not only was I not getting the increase I thought I deserved, I was being demoted.

I instructed my agent that I wanted at least the amount of money that I would have made had I continued on *The Jim Nabors Hour*. If they wanted me, they'd have to pay for me. See, it was nice to have someone do the brute work for me. It was like turning to the person in the next seat and asking, "Isn't it terrible the way Mike Tyson bit Holyfield's ear? Go in the ring and kick him in the shin for me."

My agent went back to the *Laugh-In* people and told them how much I wanted and gave them all the reasons why I was worth that much and should get that much.

He called me and said, "They listened, but they said no."

I found out that *Laugh-In* was not only creative, innovative, and funny; *Laugh-In* was also cheap.

I told him I didn't want the job.

My agent said, "Let's have breakfast."

I said, "Only if you pay. I'm out of work."

He also gave me some fast but powerful advice to digest along with the breakfast. He said, "You've only been in the business for two seasons. You've only held one job. If you disappear for a season, you may disappear forever. People forget about you. Once you're down in this business, people can be cruel."

My agent said, "Take the job for this amount. If you're good, you'll make it up along the way. But stay in the business."

I took the job and the free breakfast.

George Schlatter, the executive producer of *Laugh-In*, loved to discover new talent. He once read some jokes on a box of popcorn marketed as "Screaming Yellow Zonkers." He called whoever was called to find out about those things and learned the name of the guy who wrote most of the gags on the carton. He hired him to work on *Laugh-In*.

George was always on the lookout for new talent. His show was unique and different, so he wanted writers who were not the cookie-cutter, Hollywood writers; he searched out potential that was unique . . . and cheap.

George discovered me, but he almost discovered someone else in the process. Phyllis Diller was a guest star on *Laugh-In* and she brought along her own material. Schlatter liked the jokes, picked up Phyllis's pages, and noted the name and phone number that were handwritten on the back. It was a New York number. George called and asked, "How would you like to come to California and work on *Laugh-In*?"

The gentleman was surprised and delighted. "I'd love to," he said.

They talked in more and more detail about what would be expected, but it became apparent that they were talking about different things. George realized that he had called the number of the hair stylist that Phyllis had planned to use when she worked a gig in New York.

George told the hair-stylist that he wouldn't be working on *Laugh-In* after all. Then, he had to call Phyllis and ask who wrote those jokes. She gave him my name and number. That's when George contacted my agent and told him they wanted me, but for less than I made on my second year on *The Jim Nabors Hour*.

I started working on *Laugh-In* with a chip on my shoulder. I felt underpaid and underappreciated. I also felt that the show had taken advantage of me. They had hired me at a low salary when I was out of work. All of the other writers felt the same way—underpaid and underappreciated—probably because they *were* underpaid and underappreciated.

Most of us on the *Laugh-In* staff were inexperienced, insecure, and scared. At the beginning of our writing careers, we were certain that there had been some mistake. Things went well. We made good money and turned out funny product, but we felt it was just too good to be true. The common fear was that *they*, whoever *they* were, would discover *their* mistake, knock at our door, and proclaim, "Sorry, we got the wrong guy. You have to give all the money back, pack up your belongings, and leave town."

If someone had come to our door and said that, we'd probably have responded, "I've been expecting you." Then, we'd give the money back, pack up our stuff, and leave.

All of us on that staff had some variation of that fantasy/nightmare. We wanted to do well on the show and be better than everyone else. We were concerned about our performance and cut-throat about wishing that everyone else would do poorly.

When the Script Supervisors handed out the scripts each week, each of us would take a copy to our own private corner and count the number of jokes that we got in. It reminded me of movie cavemen each grabbing a piece of meat and hoarding it so that none of the other barbarians would steal it.

We all tried to get an edge. One writer came to work one morning and "got inspired." He started to think out loud. A joke was formulating in his brain and he wanted to let it continue, so he coaxed someone else into typing the gem while he continued to create.

He threw out a line and his cohort typed. Then, he added another line that was typed. The lines he adlibbed were good, and they kept building one upon the other. When it was done, it was a powerful joke. We were all impressed.

Then when I got home that night, I read the exact same joke in *Reader's Digest.* His entire performance in the office was to convince the rest of us that he had brilliantly conceived that joke on the spot. That's how much we wanted to better our colleagues.

We all not only wanted to get credit for our contributions but to downplay anyone else's participation. One day each week, the entire staff of twelve writers gathered to write the "Cocktail Party" jokes. (The Cocktail Party was the part of the show where everyone in the cast danced, and then action froze, while someone said something funny, which was followed by action continuing. We needed lots of gags for that segment and that's why all of us gathered to generate the material). Whenever we wrote jokes on the show, we put our initials at the top of the page. If I wrote a joke with my partner, Rowby Greeber, we put at the top of the page GPRG, which stood for Gene Perret/Rowby Greeber.   If Bill Richmond wrote a gag with Alan Katz, they typed BRAK in the upper right hand corner. That was done so the Script Supervisors could call the specific writers if they had a question or wanted some changes made.

When all twelve of us worked on the "Cocktail Party" jokes, the top of the page looked something like this:

GPRGBRAKJMDRJWJRRWJSFDML

At one of those sessions, the typist typed that at the top of the page before we had the joke written. As we were trying to come up with a new line, one of the writers, Jim Mulligan, announced that he had to leave because he had some sort of appointment before lunch. It was about 11:30. The rest of us continued.

Would it be possible to black out the initials JM from the long list of initials in this paragraph. It would seem to be more dramatic if we actually see it blacked out. I know we explain that with the next sentence, but it would be nice to actually see it. Maybe we could just overwrite it. For example -- GPRGBRAKJMDRJWJRRWJSFDML

There was also a compulsion among the young writers to always be funny. Everyone was always "on." Everyone was always doing jokes.

At lunchtime, one writer asked the waitress, "Do you accept substitutions?"

She said, "Yeah, I think so."

He said, "Then in place of the french fries, I'll have an all expense paid trip to Bermuda."

Someone else chipped in, "Do you want the suntan lotion on the side?"

The jokes were sometimes at our own expense.

Often after work, we'd gather at the SmokeHouse, the restaurant across the street from the *Laugh-In* offices, to have a cocktail or two and discuss the day's happenings. That place was a typical cocktail lounge, small tables, dark, and quiet.

One particular evening, a writer had to leave early, but the check was slow in coming. He said, "I've got to get my bill. I'm late."

I said, "Don't worry about that. I'll buy your drink." He'd only had the one.

Instead of thanking me politely, he stood up in mock rage, knocking his chair over in the process. Heads turned toward us. He pointed his finger at me and shouted, "I don't care what you say. No man should ever touch another man in that place." Then he stormed out.

Sometimes, the jokes were at my expense. I still dressed like an engineer instead of a Hollywood writer and I took some ribbing for it. Then, I bought myself a pair of really hip shoes, or at least, I thought they were hip; everyone else thought they were just funny looking. When I wore them to the *Laugh-In* offices, they became the straight line for a lot of gags.

Finally, in an effort to end the barrage of one-liners, I said, "You guys can kid about these shoes all you want, but, you know, they were given to me by my uncle on his death bed."

Another writer looked at the shoes, and then looked at me and said, "What did he die of—embarrassment?"

The ultimate in joke-after-joke exchanges happened one day when all of the writers barged into George Schlatter's office. We were going to go out to lunch together and one of the writers was already in George's office. We stopped by to see if he'd like to join us.

As soon as we walked in, the jokes started flying, good ones, bad ones, clean ones, dirty ones, and put downs of people who were there and people who weren't. Finally, when we exhausted our repertoire, we all went out to lunch.

The writer that we had walked in on was a bit grumpy. Someone asked him why. He said, "I was in with George pitching an idea for a new show and he was very interested."

We said, "That's great."

He said, "Then you clowns stormed in, tossing your jokes around, and the meeting was over. I'll never get a chance to sell this to him again."

We had no idea. Someone apologized for all of us.

Another writer said, "Why didn't you just tell us to go f--- ourselves?"

The writer said, "I think I did and somebody topped me."

Laugh-In was not only unique on screen, but off screen as well. Most variety shows that were on the air in those days taped the entire show as a single unit. They did it twice, though. They'd tape a dress rehearsal in front of a live audience followed about an hour later by the taping of the air show. *Laugh-In* worked differently. That show blocked and taped each segment of the show separately. They rehearsed one sketch, shot it, struck the set, and then worked on the next segment.

Writing procedures were different, too. We didn't have writers' offices, per se. We had apartments in a rundown motel that had been converted to permanent residences. You can imagine how classy they were when your next door neighbors were a bunch of crazy, insecure television comedy writers.

One of our Script Supervisors liked to party at night and drink, so he often slept in one of the writer's motel rooms. Several mornings, we began the day by helping him locate his car. He'd parked it somewhere in the neighborhood the night before, but could rarely remember where.

That Script Supervisor drank and his partner smoked and swallowed everything that one wasn't allowed to smoke or swallow, and they weren't too fond of one another. Again, everyone wanted to do better than everyone else, including our own writing partners.

At one party, they got into a fierce argument. One of them was cowering in a corner begging not to be shot. The other aimed a monkey wrench at him. The interesting part was that neither one of them knew it wasn't a gun that was being used. The guy holding the monkey wrench was drunk enough to think it was a gun and the one the monkey wrench was aimed at was stoned enough to think it was a gun, too. No harm was done, though. Luckily, the monkey wrench misfired.

On calmer mornings, we began the workday with our writing assignments, handed out by the above mentioned Script Supervisor/combatants. The writing assignments were a menu of the work we were expected to get done by end of day. They consisted of things like:

Three crossovers for John Wayne

Three crossovers for Raquel Welch

Five lines for the Joke Wall

A two-page sketch for Ruth Buzzi

A Big Al bit

And so on.

Each of those was a different segment of the show. Some assignments were only a single joke; some were brief bits or sketches. None of them exceeded three pages. Like the show, our writing was to be brief, punchy, and a bit wacky.

My writing partner came up with a gag that worked beautifully on the show. A husband and a wife were fighting in a living room decorated with polka dot wallpaper. The husband stormed out angrily, slammed the door, and all the polka dots fell to the floor. It was a funny sight on camera, but it was a major engineering feat. Each of the polka dots was a separate piece of material with a tiny hole in it. Then a series of pins came through the wall and supported the polka dots. When the actor slammed the door, the stagehands triggered a device that pulled the pins and the polka dots were released to the floor. It was a funny joke that cost about $5,000 to build. To amortize that set, the producer asked us to do other jokes that utilized the wall. It was practically impossible. The joke was done. It was funny, but variations couldn't be done on it.

Laugh-In also had a unique stationery situation. That was before the days of computers, so all our work had to be typed with carbon paper copies. We had paper that consisted of one sheet of normal paper with about seven carbon papers and onion skins attached. We handed in two copies to the Script Supervisors, kept a copy for our own records, and threw the other sheets away.

I wrote fast, and I liked to overwrite. If someone wanted five jokes, I wrote fifteen and let them decide which five were the best. So, if they wanted three jokes for John Wayne, I'd turn in ten.

One day, the Script Supervisor asked me to stop that. I asked why. He said, "You're wasting an awful lot of paper."

I was astounded. There was a show that was costing hundreds of thousands of dollars to produce and was generating small fortunes in income for the producers, the stars, and the network, and they wanted me to stop writing a few extra jokes because I was wasting too much paper.

I ignored the admonition because I was having good success getting jokes into the script (yes, I counted joke pages, too), and I had to be there so many hours, so I felt that I might as well be writing.

The other procedure we followed was to hand in the jokes to the Script Supervisors at the end of the day. We were to put the originals in one bin, and then put the first carbon copy in the other bin. At the end of one particular workday, I thought I had followed the procedure, and then I sat in the outer office talking to the production assistants who worked there. Our Script Supervisor, the one who often had trouble finding his car in the morning, came tearing out of his office waving pages around.

"Who handed in these jokes?" he screamed. "Who handed in these jokes?"

Since all the pages had initials at the top, there was no reason for him to ask who handed in the pages when he had the pages in his hand that had the initials at the top that would tell him who handed them in. It happened to be me who handed them in. I confessed.

He screamed at me in front of everyone, "You put the originals in the carbon paper bin and you put the carbons in the original bin."

I said to him, "I'm sorry, but if that ever happens again, here's what you should do: take these pages and move them to the other bin and take the pages that are already there and put them in the bin you took these from. That should solve your problem."

From then on, if they asked for three Lee Marvin jokes, I wrote *three* Lee Marvin jokes. If they wanted two joke wall jokes, I typed *two* joke wall jokes. No more no less. I generally finished my assignment by about 11:30 and took the rest of the day for nap time and other personal projects.

Either that or I played with my toys. My writing partner, Rowby Greeber, had fun writing letters to various people inviting them to appear on *Laugh-In*. He invited the Pope, who declined. Queen Elizabeth II also regretted that she couldn't fit it into her schedule, but he got nice letters of apology, which he saved and framed.

He also wrote to Mattel, the manufacturers of Hot Wheels, suggesting that they send some of their products that we might use as material for jokes on the show. In response, he received many of their

My *Laugh-In* writing partner, Rowby Greeber, and I reading
over the jokes we got into this week's script. You know they're
our jokes because we're laughing at them.

latest products. We had cars and tracks running throughout our motel suite, from the bedroom, through the living, and back again. They
helped fill my free time on the show.

On *The Jim Nabors Hour,* a typical script was about ¾ of an inch
thick. On *Laugh-In,* since the gags were each put on a separate page
for taping purposes, the average script was about two inches thick.
On the evening before the taping, the producer and the two Script
Supervisors finalized the script. They worked until the early morning
hours going over the script page by page, cutting, adding, and rewriting jokes. The various writing teams took turns helping out with that
process. I had to work late once every four or five weeks.

I worked one of those late night sessions with another writer who was an ass-kisser. He was devoted to getting the producer to like him and his work. At that particular session, we were going through the pages when the producer said, "I don't like page 106. Let's take it out."

This derriere-busser chimed in with, "Good idea. Let's go right from page 105 to 107."

Brilliant.

The following year, he was made a Script Supervisor.

Paul Keyes was the producer of *Laugh-In* the year when Rowan and Martin had a feud with George Schlatter and had him effectively banished from the show. Paul liked to smoke big, expensive cigars. It gave the impression that he was really in charge. At that particular late-night writing session, he handed out cigars to all of the writers there.

We all lit up and puffed away, as we reviewed the pages of the script. One writer refused; he didn't care for tobacco smoke. It didn't matter. With six others smoking stogies, he had nothing else in the room to inhale but second-hand cigar smoke.

Finally, during a short break, the non-smoker said, "Did somebody fart?"

The rest nodded their heads and said no.

He said, pleadingly, "Would somebody?"

Once the script was finalized, the writers were out of the process. We weren't invited to the taping of the shows. We weren't banned; we just weren't needed nor were we particularly welcomed. If we wanted to be there, that was okay, however, we were to just sit there like spectators, not participants.

I worked on *Laugh-In* for a full season and rarely met any of the cast members. Rowan and Martin occasionally showed up at writers' meeting to offer some input, but none of the others.

One writer dated one of the girls who was on the show. She was a gorgeous young lady, but apparently not too bright. Over dinner, that writer said to her, "You look a little pensive."

She said, "No. I'm just thinking."

That was their last date.

Laugh-In was a fun season for me because I enjoyed the zany writers I worked with. However, the show itself was not pleasant for me. I didn't feel like I was doing my best writing, nor was I allowed to. I wasted too much paper and put them in the wrong bins.

Besides, the feud hurt the morale of the staff and the quality of the show. When Dan Rowan, Dick Martin, and Paul Keyes, for whatever reasons—and they may have been justified, for all I know—forced George Schlatter off the set, the stage, and the show, much of the life went out of *Laugh-In*.

A lot of the enthusiasm went out of me. I wanted out, but I had a two-year contract with the show. If they decided to pick up my option, I would be there for another year.

However, George Schlatter was going to produce a variety show starring Bill Cosby the following season. He again offered me a contract and it was for the position of Script Supervisor on the show. It was for a hefty increase over what I was making at *Laugh-In*. My agent's advice that I'd make it up along the way turned out to be right, as it usually was. I told him to snap it up.

He did, and then he had to ask *Laugh-In* to release me from my contract. That was not an unusual happening in television; shows generally released writers who got a more promising offer. However, Dick, Dan, and Paul Keyes refused.

I was stunned. That was a great opportunity for me and they were holding me back because of their feud with George. I felt they were petty; they were using me to get revenge.

I told my agent to ask again and explain things better.

They still refused.

"We'll offer you a firm, two-year contract," Paul Keyes said.

I said, "I don't want to be here now. Why would I want to be here two years from now?" I also said, "How can you offer me a firm two years when you don't even know if the show will be renewed next season?"

Keyes said, "It doesn't matter. NBC has guaranteed Rowan and Martin that they'll be picked up for a new show even if this one doesn't come back. You'll be with that show."

I said, "No, I won't."

I turned down the two-year offer, but I still had to fulfill my contract with them. Another writer on the show had been offered a job with Cosby, but he accepted the two-year deal with *Laugh-In* instead.

I had to show up for work on *Laugh-In*. I started the previous season with a chip on my shoulder, and by that time, I showed up wearing battle gear. I didn't want to be there, and they knew I didn't want to be there. It was not a very pleasant situation for me.

During our third week of pre-production, Paul Keyes called all the writers to a meeting in his office. We were going to audition a new cast member for the upcoming season—a ventriloquist. He and his dummy did part of their act. They adlibbed, they were very entertaining, and we were all impressed.

I had a terrific headache, though. I asked Paul's receptionist if she had any aspirin. She didn't.

After the audition, we took a brief break before we got on with the writers' meeting. I just laid my head on the table.

When Paul Keyes returned after a restroom break, he said to me, "Did you ever see two characters work so well together before?"

I said, "Yeah, Ernest Borgnine and Ethel Merman."

I was doing a joke because they had a very brief but stormy marriage a few years before. Incidentally, I had stolen the joke from my former writing partner, Arnie Kogen.

Paul Keyes exploded. He called me a few choice names before the meeting continued.

The next morning, my agent called and said, "I don't know what the hell you did, but you've been released from your contract. You've been fired. Congratulations."

Later that day, I signed with George Schlatter and the Cosby show.

As a postscript, *Laugh-In* was cancelled after that season. As I understood it, Rowan and Martin were paid off by NBC instead of being given another show. The other writer—the one who was enticed to stay with the offer of a firm, two-year commitment—never got the second year of his *firm*, two-year contract.

Chapter Eleven
The New Bill Cosby Show

George Schlatter not only hired me as a writer on the Cosby show, but he hired me as Script Supervisor. In theory, that meant I was the head writer. In reality, it meant absolutely nothing. George Schlatter was the real head-writer. He decided what went into the show, how it should be rewritten, and how it should be polished. So, I was just one of the writers on the show—the one with the most desirable office and with the Script Supervisor title in the closing credits. That looked good on my resume and I hoped that it might help me get a real head-writer job further down the line.

Even with my exalted title, working for Bill Cosby caused me some trepidation. My background and training was as a gag-writer, a joke man, a one-liner guy. Bill Cosby didn't do one-liners, and I really had no training in sketch writing. The veterans on *The Jim Nabors Hour* did most of the longer sketches, and *Laugh-In* didn't do anything longer than three pages. There was good reason for me to be apprehensive.

Bill Cosby, though, put my mind at ease immediately. When we had our first scripts typed, bound, and delivered to the office, Cosby came in for a writers meeting. He picked up the box of scripts that we had worked so hard on. They were supposed to be distributed so we could mark them with notes for the rewrites, but he dumped them into the trash. We assumed that meant he didn't like parts of them. With that emphatic gesture, he said, "I'm not Bob Hope and I'm not *Laugh-In*." That, of course, made me, who had written for both Bob Hope and *Laugh-in*, feel most welcome. Perhaps that firm two years with Rowan and Martin didn't seem that bad after all.

Cosby was right, though. He wasn't *Laugh-In* and he wasn't Bob Hope. In our first draft of the first show, we obviously hadn't captured what Bill or the show was all about. Cosby had always been hilariously funny, but in a non-traditional way. Much of his appeal was that he was different from the other comedians. He wasn't Hope, Henny Youngman, or even Lenny Bruce. He was Bill Cosby. We, as writers, had to find that voice.

It wasn't difficult, really. When I had an idea for a monologue, I met with Bill and told him the basic idea. Bill was such a comedy genius that he immediately began dissecting the premise for funny angles. He tossed out ideas off the top of his head. He presented other comedic aspects of the basic premise. I discovered that if I paid close attention and took good notes, I could go to my typewriter and create a funny monologue by following the outline that Bill gave me.

The sketch writing technique came more slowly, but it came. I really learned sketch writing on the Cosby show. We turned out a lot of material and we rejected much of it. Nonetheless, writing that many sketches was good training.

I shared an office and most of the writing with a writer from England named Ray Taylor. Ray was a creative writer who liked to go for the off-beat or unusual. He suggested an idea about a mannequin that came to life in a store window. I liked the concept and we wrote it together for the first show of the season.

Cosby liked it, too. It wasn't *Laugh-In* and it wasn't Bob Hope. It was unique.

Normally, the writers watched the taping of the show together on a monitor in a backstage room. That way, we could discuss what was working and what wasn't and have notes prepared for the between-shows meeting. However, Ray and I wanted to be by the stage when the mannequin sketch was performed. We wanted to hear the laughter and the applause. We felt we should be close by in case the audience rose to their feet and demanded that the authors make an appearance.

We stood off to the side of the audience seats. In fact, I was leaning against the grandstand that held the audience, my elbow near some-one's feet. The sketch began. When Bill, who played the mannequin, first showed signs of being alive, the audience chuckled. That's about as much laughter as the sketch got. It went downhill from that open-ing titter, and then it died.

Ray and I stood there stunned. It was supposed to be a smash. It was written to be dynamite. Bill Cosby thought it would get gales of laughter. Instead, it just died.

There was a gentleman in the audience whose feet were near my elbow. He turned to his wife and said as a matter of fact, "It was a *good* idea."

Ray and I went across the street to the City Slicker to drown our bruised egos. It didn't appear that we would be called upon to take the stage for any bows that evening.

Ray was an enjoyable office partner because he had a delightful way with understatement. Once, we were working on a sketch about Bill and his onstage wife. As we were trying to write, I adlibbed a few lines of dialogue. I was using the voice of the wife and I said something very romantic. I put all my acting skills into the delivery of the line and I delivered it to Ray in the hope that he would accept it and type it into the script. Instead, he looked at me without changing his expression and said, "That's your seductive attitude, I presume?"

Often Ray's barbs went completely undetected. We had Groucho Marx as a guest on the show late in the season—actually too late to save the ratings and the show, and too late for Groucho, too. At that time, Groucho was past his peak—way past. He had enjoyed a comeback of sorts as a camp act with the college crowd, but he definitely was not up to performing very well.

Erin Fleming was Groucho's escort and advisor, whether he wanted or needed advice or not. Once, I saw a television report on the premier of Marlon Brando's new film, *Last Tango in Paris*. That was a controversial film because it was sexually graphic. After the premier, the reporters interviewed some of the celebrities leaving the theatre after the first showing. The inside thing to do was praise the picture, speak out against censorship, and all that stuff.

The interviewer asked Groucho Marx what he thought of the film. He said, "Worst film I ever saw in my life. Terrible."

Suddenly, Erin noticed that he was on camera and she whispered to him.

Groucho then said, "It was great."

That seemed to be the influence she exerted on the feeble star.

The joke going around our offices was that Erin wanted to be part of Groucho's family so much that she was thinking of having her name changed legally to "Flemmo."

One morning we came to work to find that Erin was in our office and frantically making telephone calls to the east coast. She was very upset about the fact that Groucho was not going to be receiving a special Oscar at the upcoming Academy Awards show; instead, Edward G. Robinson was to be the honoree.

Erin called Woody Allen from our office to complain. Woody said that Robinson was very sick and that was why the Academy was honoring him now. She called others, but could get no satisfaction. In desperation, she sat there talking to Ray Taylor and I. "I can't understand why they didn't give this Oscar to Groucho. I think I must have screwed every member of the committee."

Ray said quietly, "Perhaps you've answered your own question."

She never got the irony.

It may have dawned on her later, though, because she did cause us some grief when Groucho was a guest on the show. We had rehearsed the entire show and Groucho seemed happy with the material. Then, we got a call after he got home that he wasn't happy with the material. I recalled that scene after *Last Tango in Paris*. Maybe "Flemmo" changed his opinion again.

George Schlatter set up a luncheon meeting for the next day. George and I would have lunch at Groucho Marx's house to discuss changes in the script. Even though that was a problem for the show, I was thrilled to be having lunch at the home of the legendary Groucho Marx.

Groucho had many fine writers working with him in his hey-day—Max Kauffman and S. J. Perlman among them. It would be great, I thought, to ask the comedian's thoughts about them.

After our meeting and while we were waiting for lunch to be served, I did work up the courage to ask Groucho. "You've had some great writers working for you over the years," I said. "Could you give me your impression of some of them?"

Groucho said, "We never had any good writers. My brothers and I came up with all the funny ideas."

I said, "What are we having for lunch?"

On the Cosby show, I got to work with Pat McCormick, one of the fabled, wacky characters of Hollywood. Pat was a bright, funny, creative writer and performer. He played the big, rich man who partnered with the diminutive Paul Williams character to back Burt Reynolds's in *Cannonball Run*, the hit comedy movie. Pat was a big man with no inhibitions. He'd say or do anything. He was famous for his pants dropping. Reportedly, he did it while gazing up at Michelangelo's painting in the Sistine Chapel and at his own mother's funeral. Those stories may be apocryphal, but that's the sort of character he was—one that would support such myths. Pat was a minor celebrity that the major celebrities liked to have around because he was so goofy he was fun.

McCormick and his writing partner on the show shared an office next to mine with an adjoining door between the two. While Ray and I were working on a comedy sketch one time, we decided we needed a bizarre line, the kind McCormick specialized in.

I told Ray, "I'll get Pat to put a line in there for us." There was no way I was prepared for the scene that greeted me when I opened the adjoining door. Pat's partner was seated at his desk typing. Pat Mc-Cormick, all six-foot, six-inches of him, was pacing back and forth, smoking a huge cigar and wearing a derby hat, but nothing else.

He said, "May we help you?"

I said, "I'll come back later" and got the hell out of there.

Bobby Fisher was making the front pages of all the papers while I worked on the Cosby show. He was competing for the world championship of chess against the reigning champion from Russia, Boris Spassky. The match was front page news all across the nation and probably the world.

Ray Jessel, a writer on our staff, claimed to be a pretty fair chess player. Of course, Pat McCormick challenged him. One day, a match between Ray and Pat was arranged that would rival the world championship match. Even though most of us knew little about chess, we all gathered in the front office to watch the confrontation. They set up the board and flipped a coin to see who would play first. McCormick won the honors.

He pondered the board for a few seconds and moved one of his pawns out two spaces. Ray retaliated by moving one of his pawns. Pat shouted, "There's no way I can beat you now," took off his cowboy boot, and tossed it through the large plate glass window that opened onto Beverly Boulevard.

Ray apparently won by default.

Pat wrote strange, bizarre, off-beat, but insidiously funny lines— the kind that could be used on television and the kind that couldn't. One night, he and I were working at NBC. To the side of the freeway near the NBC Burbank studios was a building with a sign that read, "The Braille Institute." As Pat and I were leaving the studios on the way back to Hollywood, we passed that building at about two o'clock in the morning. Of course, the sign was unlighted and all of the windows were dark. Pat noticed that all the lights were out and said, "That's a shame, those poor people must be working late tonight."

There was another writer on the Cosby staff who insisted he was taller than Pat. In fact, that writer felt he was richer than most, more talented than all, more experienced than the rest, and had no compunction about telling each and every one of us that he was.

My office mate on the show, Ray Taylor, was from London. He worked there many years as a writer and as a television and radio personality. Several of us Cosby writers were at lunch one day when another person on the show came over to talk to us. He said relatives were visiting and would soon be on their way to London. He asked Ray to recommend some nice restaurants in London.

This blowhard writer, who thought he knew more about London than the natives, fielded the question. "Do they want to see celebrities?" he asked. Then, he went on without waiting for a reply. "If they want to see celebrities tell them to go to . . . ." He mentioned some London restaurant. "Big celebrities are always there," he said. "One night, Ringo Starr was at one table. Michael Caine was at the next table. I'm at another table . . . ." He raised self-enhancement to new heights, whether he had reason to or not.

Several of us on the Cosby staff volunteered our writing services for a huge charity show that was produced in Hollywood each year. We had a production meeting one evening at the home of Jack Haley,

Jr. Before the meeting got underway, the writer in question challenged me to a game of 8-ball pool. I had a billiards table in my home at that time and played quite a bit. My game at that time was above average.

I handled my colleague pretty easily. I beat him five or six games in a row. I said, "Another game?"

He said, "Naw. I don't want to play anymore." He didn't concede, mind you; he just grew weary of the game.

Instead, he said to me, who had just trimmed his clock for the past half an hour, "Would you like me to teach you some trick shots?"

I was proud of *The New Bill Cosby Show*. It was well-written, but it wasn't successful. When the ratings came out each week, we kidded that our show had an asterisk after it that meant it was "staff-watched." Not many people tuned in to see it. Of course, a few years later, Bill Cosby did manage to get a few people to watch his sitcom.

Ronnie Graham wrote some wonderful musical pieces for the show, we did some nice opening monologues for Cosby, and the sketches were innovative and funny. Of course, George Schlatter added his own wacky imprint to each show. It was a funny variety show, just not popular.

The most memorable show to me was the one on which Peter Sellers and Lily Tomlin were guests. Lily did a "Hi, Honey, I'm Home" sketch with Bill that was hilarious. She played the wife who rebelled against all the housework she had to do while her husband was at the office.

Lily also teamed up with Peter Sellers in an airline sketch that began with the pilot announcing a crisis. He told all the passengers to prepare for a crash landing and to follow the instructions of the flight attendants.

Peter Sellers turned to Lily, who was seated beside him, and asks if she was in the correct seat.

She replied by asking, "What's the difference? We're going to crash. Who cares what seats we're in?"

Sellers explained, "I think we should switch because, you see, your life is passing before my eyes."

The rest of the sketch was them reviewing each other's lives. They were attracted to each other in the airport, but were both too timid to do anything about it. They fell in love. Then, the danger passed and they reverted to being quiet, non-communicative seat mates again.

The biggest sketch of the show featured Bill Cosby as an old butler at a political embassy. Peter Sellers played all of the other parts, including a delegate from India, who was a snake charmer and carried his pets in one of his satchels, a British politician, who insisted on a certain type of tea and also drank a touch too much Beefeaters gin, and one or two others with their own peculiar quirks.

Bill, as the old butler, was so senile that he kept sending them into the wrong rooms and causing all sorts of confusion and hilarity.

It was a beautifully-written show, and of course, with Sellers, Tomlin, and Cosby, it was also magnificently performed.

George Schlatter liked the show, but chided us writers. He was upset at the cost of the embassy piece. Since Sellers played all the roles and had extensive makeup for each character, the segments had to be shot separately and then assembled in editing. That much editing time was expensive. George told us, "Don't ever hand in another sketch like that. As I watched the editing time mounting up, it reminded me of filling my boat with fuel. I kept hearing that ding-ding-ding that meant more money."

It amused all of us writers that Schlatter was trying to garner some sympathy by telling us how expensive it was to fill his boat with petrol when none of us could afford a boat in the first place.

Expensive or not, it was a well-written show. I had to defend it a few weeks later when we had a show that wasn't working as well as the Peter Sellers-Lily Tomlin script. One network executive remarked, "The writing is letting us down."

I said, "Wait a minute, how about the writing on the Peter Sellers-Lily Tomlin show?"

He replied, "When you have performers that great, you can't do anything wrong."

That was the usual philosophy in Hollywood. When it was great, the performers got the credit; when it was pedestrian, the writers got the blame.

Cosby had a brilliant and funny writing staff. Admittedly though, we were sometimes our funniest and most brilliant when we weren't at the typewriter. The apex of the craziness happened one day when one of our writers had a luncheon date with a recent Playboy centerfold. The rest of us knew she was coming and we did our research. We bought the issue she was featured in and passed it around the office so we could all enjoy her in her nude glory.

When she arrived at the offices, we learned she was as gorgeous dressed as she was naked. See-through blouses were in vogue at that time, and she was dressed in vogue. What we viewed in the magazine earlier, we could see just as plainly through her blouse. Both views were enjoyable.

The writer had made arrangements to take the young lady to lunch at a restaurant just across Beverly Boulevard from our offices. It was a newly opened restaurant called Dubrovnik. So, we all decided to have lunch there, too, because it was convenient and because a see-through blouse was a terrible thing to waste. We all piled in and were our show-off funniest. I'll skip most of the lunchtime humor because it had that "you had to be there" ring to it, but at the end of lunch, Pat McCormick stood on one of the tables in his boxer shorts.

He announced, "I'm buying lunch, but I don't have my wallet with me. I'm leaving my trousers here as a good faith down payment." He stuck his trousers up into the lattice work that decorated the ceiling.

The owner of the restaurant got very upset and rushed over to our table.   He spoke with a heavy accent. "Meester MeeCormick, Meester MeeCormick, what are you doing?"

Pat said, "I guess you're not using to dealing with us circus folk, are you?"

Pat got down, grabbed the half empty bottle of wine from the table, and began to exit, while his trousers were still wedged in the ceiling. Laughing hysterically, we all followed him outside. The frustrated owner didn't think it was funny.

"Meester MeeCormick, you cannot take the wine. You cannot take the wine."

Pat just kept walking in his boxer shorts across Beverly Boulevard.

"I will lose my license Meester MeeCormick. Please . . . I will lose my license."

Pat paid no attention.

The owner grabbed the bottle of wine and tried to wrest it from Pat's grip. That was in the middle of Beverly Boulevard, a very heavily traveled road. As they tugged back and forth, the rest of us stood on the sidewalk laughing.

Finally, one of our writers, who only was about five-feet, two-inches tall, threw a shawl over his head and began crossing the street, completely blind. Cars zoomed to a halt. It looked like a Mexican blanket with feet crossing the street.

Ronnie Graham, who wrote the musical numbers for the show, had broken his leg in a motorcycle accident, and he was in a cast and on crutches. He hobbled out into the middle of Beverly Boulevard, where McCormick and the restaurant proprietor were still tugging at the bottle of wine. Ronnie shouted loudly, "I can walk! I can walk!" Then, he threw his crutches across the boulevard, raised his arms heavenward, and fell flat on his ass.

I ran across the street and hurried into the safety of the Cosby Show offices before the authorities arrived or someone got killed.

I'm not sure whether that Playboy centerfold ever dated another television comedy writer or not.

The show was fun, but it was doomed. It lasted that one season. My next gig was on the picket line.

Chapter Twelve
On Strike

I was making more money than I ever thought I would. The Guild decreed that we should be making more, so they went on strike. We writers couldn't work, we didn't get paid, we were not permitted to negotiate for future work, and we had to walk a picket line. I walked outside of Universal Studios. I had never been in Universal Studios, but I paraded in front of it trying to keep other people from going in.

Everyone who belonged to the Guild had to walk the picket line. No excuses were accepted. One day, I walked beside a very nice, older woman. We carried our signs in typical unionized boredom. As we walked, we conversed and I asked her what kind of writing she did. She informed me that she wasn't a writer. She worked for a major star. He sent his maid to do his picket carrying chores.

One morning, as we dutifully circled the gate in front of one of Universal's entrances, Carroll O'Connor drove by in a beautiful Rolls Royce. Carroll O'Connor was the actor who played Archie Bunker on *All In the Family*. He braked at the guard house and then a loud discussion began. Apparently, Carroll O'Connor was quite upset that he would not be allowed to park his car in Universal's lot while he came out and picketed their studio for being unfair to writers.

Some of those incidents might have seemed funnier to me if my circumstances weren't decidedly unfunny. The Cosby show had not been renewed, so I was out of work.

There was some talk about a job offer from *The Carol Burnett Show*. I told my agent that a strike was imminent, so we should wrap up negotiations. He assured me that even though I couldn't work on the show during the strike, he could surely negotiate a contract for me.

He was wrong.

We found out that negotiations were forbidden during strikes, too.

I had no work, no prospects, and no income. Walking in a circle for two hours every morning was not fun for me.

Other people didn't make it any more fun, either. One morning, we circled near a bus stop bench. A woman watched us walking around carrying our picket signs that proclaimed that the studios were unfair to writers. She was eating from a little bag of sunflower seeds.

Finally, as her bus was approaching, she spoke to us. "How much do you make for writing a show?" she asked.

I said, "I'm not exactly sure," I responded. "I think it's about $10,000."

Her eyes widened in disbelief. "For a half-hour of work?" she asked.

"Well, it's not really a half-hour of work," I said. I was going to go on and explained that it takes many hours of meetings, writing, and rewriting to produce a half-hour of television comedy.

She would hear none of that. Her bus arrived and she had to get on, but she glared at me in anger. Before getting on the bus, she threw the bag of sunflower seeds at me. The doors closed and she rode off, satisfied that she had done her bit to retaliate against greedy television scribes.

Another morning a truck stopped at a red light near the Universal gate I was picketing. The driver glanced toward us and gave a raised fist salute—one union brother offering support for another. All of us acknowledged his greeting. The truck driver shouted over to us, "What are you guys striking for?"

I personally had no idea. Being a relative newcomer to the industry, I didn't get too involved in union proceedings. I was just happy to be included in the membership. It delighted me to be allowed to enter those hallowed studios, so I certainly didn't want to antagonize them. I was a kid locked in a candy store. First, let me savor the candy before you give me a lecture on how bad sugar is for the teeth and overall health.

I had no idea what we were striking for, but part of it must have been money. It always was.

So I shouted back to my brother in the labor movement, "More money."

Just then, the light turned green. However, before driving off he shouted back, "You want more money for that crap you write?"

So much for union loyalty.

One young gentleman approached a group of us, as we ambled around, supposedly fiercely protesting studio injustice to writers.

"You guys writers?" he asked.

We said we were.

"I'm a writer, too," he told us.

He went on. "I haven't sold anything yet, but I'm taking a course over at the Writers Guild."

"Wonderful," we said.

He told us who was teaching the course. The teacher was a well-established, well-known, and well-respected writer. Some of my fellow picketers knew that gentleman personally; others of us knew him by reputation.

The young man said, "I wrote a script that he said was pretty good."

"That's great," we said.

Our new friend went and retrieved a copy of the script from his car. Probably he figured we wouldn't believe his tale unless he showed us the words on the page.

"Here it is," he said.

We just looked at it. It's very hard to picket and read at the same time, besides I wasn't at all sure that we might not be in violation of Guild rules if we read a script during the strike. There was no point in taking any chances.

The aspiring writer said, "The instructor told me that it needed a few changes, and if I did a rewrite, he might be able to show it to some friends and maybe get me a sale."

"That's terrific," we all agreed.

The youngster said, "Yeah, well, if he wants me to do any work on this script, he's going to have to pay me."

As the aspiring writer walked off with the imperfect, but nearly viable script under his arm, I thought to myself that I'd probably never meet him in any of the writers meetings.

I never have met him.

Of course, I don't remember his name or what he looked like. He may have sold several scripts and become the head of some studio, for all I know.

He wanted to be paid while he learned how to write. I had already learned some things. I wanted to get that strike over with and get paid for having already learned how to write.

But, no, I just kept walking in circles . . . walking in circles . . . walking in circles.

Chapter Thirteen
The Carol Burnett Show

The strike ended, not so much happily as predictably. We writers got some of what we wanted and some of what we didn't want. The producers gave us some of what we thought we had coming to us and some of what they thought we had coming to us. So, it was a compromise that we fought hard for and won . . . or lost.

The strange thing about writers' strikes is that a good percentage of the Guild members also have production companies. In effect, many of us picket ourselves. We carry signs that should read, "I'm unfair to me." However, in the end, it somehow makes sense, and the Guild does an awful lot of good for its members.

The good, post-strike news from my agent was that Carol Burnett's people did indeed want me. The bad, post-strike news was they wanted me for a lot less than I wanted them to want me for. In fact, they wanted me for only about half of what I wanted them to want me for.

I told my agent, "I can't accept an offer that low." No other offers were forthcoming as yet, but that one was unacceptable.

My agent asked his usual question: "Are you prepared to lose it?"

I said, "Yes."

My agent said, "I'll talk to them again. Personally, I think there must be a misunderstanding."

He went back to the Burnett people and came back with some good, post-strike news. There was a misunderstanding. They had me mixed up with someone else they wanted. They doubled their offer.

We negotiated from that point and I finally got an offer I could accept.

So, I went to work for *The Carol Burnett Show.*

Carol had been on the air for six seasons. It never did great in the ratings, but it never did that badly, either. It was a good show, respected by the viewers and by the industry. The sixth season, though, was problematic for them. During that year, they had both a producing team and a head-writing team. Apparently, they were adversarial. The writers had a problem about which team they should pay allegiance to and whether they should follow the producers' orders and irritate the head-writers, or do what the head-writers wanted and annoy the producers. It became such turmoil that Carol got rid of the producers and most of the writing staff after that sixth season. That was when I came in—with the new wave.

Ed Simmons was hired as the new producer/head-writer. He took all of the writing staff to lunch one day in order to wine us, dine us, and give us the company line. "We're going to stand together this year. When one person writes a good sketch, we all wrote it. When someone writes a bad sketch, we all wrote it. Morale among the writers will be very high this year because we're going to work as a team."

After the lunch, Ed and I stayed on for a post-luncheon drink at the bar. "Good luck" I said to Ed, meaning that I listened to his spiel, but I never believed it would work. He assured me that he was sincere and that he would hold himself and us to his words.

God bless him, he did. *The Carol Burnett Show* was a delight to work on.

Of course, Simmons didn't manage to keep all of his State of the Staff promises. When we went to work, he told us that one of his goals for the upcoming season was to never lose a sketch. "Once a sketch goes into the show, it stays there," he vowed.

The very first sketch we wrote for the very first show was cut at the very first writers meeting after the very first run-through. My partner and I wrote the sketch.

Joe Hamilton, Carol's husband and executive-producer of the show, said, "The 'Evel Knievel' sketch is out." He said it in a way that left no room for discussion.

My heart broke and I was a bit angry internally. I couldn't express it externally because I was a frightened young writer who was happy to be working, especially on a prestigious show like *The Carol Burnett Show*. I wasn't about to become confrontational.

Joe further explained, "That sketch was never any damn good."

On the drive home, I thought, that sketch was put into the script, read on Monday, rehearsed for three days, and dropped just two days before the show aired. If it was "never any damn good," I had to wonder who picked it, put it in the show, and sent it to the typists. So, I got even more offended at his tirade.

The next day, I went back to work and took it like a man. I had no power to do anything else.

Ed Simmons must have felt like a pitcher who throws a home run ball on his first pitch to the plate and then curses, "Damn it, there goes my no-hitter."

Bill Richmond and I had worked together on the staff at *Laugh-In,* but we didn't work as a team on that show. We were paired up on the Burnett Show. One question was who would get top billing. I kind of felt that "Perret and Richmond" had more of a rhythm to it than "Richmond and Perret." Richmond may have felt the opposite.

Anyway, Ed Simmons came into our office one day and tossed a coin. I called it in the air and lost. We were listed on the credits as "Bill Richmond and Gene Perret." However, I insisted that with all great comedy teams, the funny one got bottom billing. Dean Martin and Jerry Lewis, Abbott and Costello, Burns and Allen . . . and "Bill Richmond and Gene Perret." The real comedy talent came last. It was my petulant form of rationalization and revenge.

Despite my billing setback, the Burnett show was ideal for a writer for many reasons. First, it was a terrifically talented staff that worked together and got along well, thanks to Ed Simmons' leadership. Everyone pulled together and there were few problems when someone offered suggestions for a sketch or even worked on a rewrite of a sketch. So long as the material was funny when it aired, we stayed happy.

Second, the show was well-respected by the viewers and the industry. That was rare in television. We used to kid that when we went to a party and people asked, "What do you do for a living?" We answered that we were accountants. Saying that we were television writers would prompt the next question, "What show do you write for?" When we told them, the questioner would inevitably say, "I hate that show." Most viewers pretended to hate every show. As a staff writer on the Burnett show, though, we were proud to say we wrote for it. People liked that show.

Third, the show had a very talented cast and they respected the script. Much of the attitude of a show came from the star, and Carol was very fair with the writers. The cast and the director gave the script the benefit of the doubt every time. Even when the writing was weak, they'd give it 110 percent and add little bits that improved it.

Harvey Korman had a reputation as somewhat of a whiner on the show, but his complaints were neither harmful nor malicious. It was almost like a pleasant hobby for him.

At the end of each season, the show would throw a huge party with dinner and drinks in one of the rehearsal halls followed by what we called "The Flip Show" in the studio. The Flip Show was emceed by Carol Burnett and anyone on the show was free to present a sketch, a musical piece, a comedy bit, or whatever would satirize the season. It was a great, fun way to end the show for the year.

Ed Simmons did a routine in which he read from his diary as producer of the show. He said of Harvey: "July 15th... Harvey came into my office and complained that he didn't have enough to do on the show. August 15th... Harvey came into my office and complained that he had too much to do on the show. September 15th... Harvey came into my office and complained that everything was OK."

One writer from a previous season mentioned that the Burnett cast always added to the script and made it even better than it was on paper. Many on that writing staff were offended by the remark. They wanted *all* the credit for brilliant sketches to go to the writing staff. They objected to actors stealing part of their thunder. However, I thought the remark was perfectly valid. The performers did make the sketches better. That's what they were supposed to do.

In order to produce a quality show, writing and performing should fuse into a solid presentation. Neither one can excel without the other. Once they fuse, it's almost impossible to tell whose input produced what. It's like making Jell-O, you mix water with a powder, chill it, and you have a solid, jiggling mass. Once that mass sets up, though, it's impossible to define which part is water and which part is powder. That's the same with a quality comedy presentation.

Thanks to Carol's example, I believe the performers never criticized the writers for a weak script. They got pedestrian sketches from time to time, but they realized that the material couldn't be superb every time. When the writing was under par, they accepted that as part of producing a weekly variety show. They asked us to improve it as much as we could, and we often worked long hours to make a weak sketch stronger, and they worked on it themselves at rehearsals. Sometimes, we saved it; other times, we couldn't. It was never taken personally, though. They knew we weren't trying to kill their careers or sabotage the show, as some performers on other shows felt.

Fourth, as a writer, we created any wacky character or premise we wanted. One week, Harvey played a werewolf, and the next week, he played a distinguished actor. Tim could be a buffoon or a poor creature taking on dog-like characteristics after being bitten by his girl's schnauzer. Each sketch we wrote was new and unique. On sitcoms, of course, we were limited by the characters. Archie Bunker would always be Archie Bunker; Lucy and Ricky and Fred and Ethel would always be Lucy and Ricky and Fred and Ethel. It was easy to get tired of the people and the premises. On *The Carol Burnett Show,* each premise was different. The people populating the sketches changed from week to week. The writers were the ones changing them, and that made the job less monotonous than most and much more fun.

Fifth, the *network suits* left us alone. The show was never very highly rated, yet it was high enough and respected enough to be re-newed each year. The execs wanted to hang around and tamper with the top-rated shows. Consequently, since we traditionally came in at around twentieth position each week in the ratings, they weren't too involved with us. Also, Carol's prestige and Joe Hamilton's toughness discouraged *the suits* from getting too involved with our show. We ran it ourselves, and that was always more pleasant.

Bill Richmond and I were very prolific on the show, and our work was highly regarded by the head-writer, the executive producer, and the cast. Later, when Carol and Joe Hamilton wanted to syndicate the show, they asked the writers to take half of their contracted residual fees. I objected. "We have a contract that spells out our residual fees." I said. "Why not abide by it?"

Their representative explained that they were pioneering an at-tempt to transform a one-hour variety show into a half-hour format for syndication. It was risky. They could lose money.

I said, "But if it's successful and makes money, then you get to keep most of it, while we still get paid at the lesser rate." They were asking us to finance their risk, yet allow them to reap most of the prof-its. To me, it didn't seem fair.

They understood our complaint and we compromised. Ed Sim-mons was to make a list of who wrote what for each individual show. If a writer's work was represented on any given show, that writer would get paid the full, contracted residual. If a writer had nothing on that particular show, the writer would be compensated at half of the contracted residual.

Bill Richmond and I were represented on almost every show.

However, we also "killed somebody off" on every show, too. Whenever we needed a sketch ending, we seemed to go for the ultimate—we assassinated Tim Conway's character. Usually, we ended our sketches with devastating explosions. We became known on the staff as "The Boom-Boom Boys."

At one time, we had a sign outside our office proclaiming that nickname for all visitors to see. CBS, though, wasn't happy with that advertisement, so they kept taking the sign down. We put it up a few times more, but eventually we caved in to their wishes and left the sign off.

At one point, though, we must have had conscience attacks because we vowed never to end our sketches with deaths again. It was tough, but we adhered to our self-censorship.

The staff in general was liberal with the life of Tim Conway's characters. We terminated Tim often. Two writers once said that if you had an ending to a sketch, then writing the sketch was easy. The executive producer said, "Okay, Tim dies at the end. Have the sketch on my desk by 4:30."

Rudy DeLuca and Barry Levinson once wrote a sketch that featured Carol Burnett and Tim Conway as husband and wife staying in a motel room. While they were in bed, trying to sleep, Carol heard a bug in the room. She wanted Tim to get rid of it. Tim put a glass over the bug, which supposedly would keep it immobilized and out of harm's way for the rest of the night. When they tried to go back to sleep, the glass shattered. Apparently the insect, which was never actually seen on camera, was strong enough to move the glass. Other complications kept the sketch moving, and it was funny.

We needed an ending, though. The first ending written was that

Tim put the bug outside the motel room door. Then Carol felt badly about exiling a bug and forcing him to live away from his wife and children. She cajoled Tim into going outside to check on the bug. When he opened the door and stepped outside, the sound effects man produced a loud "crunch." Tim had stepped on the insect ending the sketch.

We writers winced. "You can't end a sketch like that," we said. "The viewers will turn against us." It was interesting that we could kill Tim Conway off two or three times each week, but we couldn't bring ourselves to destroy an unseen, anonymous insect.

On our own, with no complaints from the censors, the network, or the producer, we writers worked on a new ending.

The new one that the team came up with was probably better than the original anyway. At Carol's prompting, Tim went outside to make sure that the critter was all right. Tim did step outside the room, out of camera range. He came back in and assured Carol that the bug family was safe and happy outside the motel room. She was pleased. Then, as Tim climbed into bed, he turned his back to the camera and we saw a giant lizard attached to the back of his pajamas. He climbed into bed and the lights went out. We ended the sketch knowing that soon all hell would break loose again in that motel room.

Sketch endings gave us Burnett writers our biggest headaches. On that show, the endings had to be crisp, concise, logical, and most of all, funny. The finale of each piece on the show was like the punch line of a joke. It had to be powerful and effective. Otherwise, the entire sketch would seem flat.

When we writers handed in a first draft of a comedy sketch for consideration, it often came back to us with notes and recommendations for a rewrite. Invariably, one of the suggestions was, "It needs a better ending."

My writing partner and I generally felt that the ending we handed in with the sketch was the optimum finish. Any new ending we created would be a compromise, as far as we were concerned.

Eventually, we devised a deceptive plan to outsmart the authorities. We wrote our sketch with the ending that we felt was appropriate and powerful. However, we didn't turn that finish in with our first draft. Instead, we'd create an alternate, less effective finale. That's the one we submitted with our original pages.

When the decision makers returned the piece for a rewrite with the inevitable "It needs a better ending" notation, we *pretended* to struggle with it creatively. After a reasonable amount of time, we'd simply take our original, preferred ending out of the drawer, attach it to our sketch as the improved, freshly created, new finish, and turn it back in. It worked just about every time.

Naughty, we admit, but clever.

Two of my favorite sketches that my partner and I wrote during our five years on the Burnett Show were "No-Frills Airline" and "The Hollow Hero."

"No-Frills Airline" was Carol Burnett's idea. On the first day of production after our hiatus, Carol spoke with Bill and me about the idea of airlines offering cheaper flights. For a minimum fee, you could get on the plane but would get no meals or other luxuries. She thought it was a funny idea and would make good sketch material. We agreed and offered to write the piece.

With Carol as the flight attendant, Harvey Korman as the full-paying passenger, and Tim Conway as the no-frills flyer, it turned out to be a hilarious piece.

"The Hollow Hero" happened as a result of Bill Richmond reading a book by F. A. Rockwell called "How To Write Plots That Sell." Chapter Three in that book is entitled "Jokes as a Goldmine of Plots." Using an old joke as a framework, we created the Hollow Hero character, and of course, gave birth to Carol's parody of a queen.

This sketch worked beautifully on stage. In fact, at the meeting between the dress rehearsal taping and the air show, Joe Hamilton announced, "We're not going to do the 'Hollow Hero' sketch again."

Carol said, "Oh, yes we are."

Joe argued, "But we've got it in the can. It worked perfectly and it doesn't need any improvements."

Carol said, "It's not often we get a piece of material that is that much fun to perform. We're going to do it again."

We did it again and it worked magnificently a second time.

However, what made that one of my favorite sketches from the show was the writing of it. Bill and I wrote it in one morning and we laughed during the entire process. Each line in the sketch was a laugh generator. We laughed as we wrote it. The other writers laughed when we read it to them. It was just great fun to assemble. The fact that it generated laughs on stage also was a fringe benefit. [NOTE: both of the above sketches are printed in their entirety in Gene Perret's book, *The New Comedy Writing Step by Step* (Quill Driver Books, 2007)]

Of course, the most memorable sketch from *The Carol Burnett Show* was "Went with the Wind." It was a take-off on the classic film, *Gone with the Wind*, and featured that bit that's shown on television anytime there's a documentary about Carol Burnett or the show. It shows Carol coming down the stairs wearing not only the drapes from the window, but also the curtain rod that came with them. Rick Hawkins and Liz Sage wrote that sketch entirely and it was brilliant. I had nothing to do with it except to enjoy it as we watched it being taped. I also enjoy cashing the residual checks that arrive each time a clip from it airs on television.

Another memorable facet of *The Carol Burnett Show* was the laughter between Harvey Korman and Tim Conway. People want to know if it was real or if we wrote it into the script. It was always real. Tim Conway's purpose in life was to make Harvey Korman laugh.

One notable example was a sketch called "The Drum Out." Korman was to be expelled from the military. In disgrace, as the drums rolled, he would be stripped of all military insignias and banished from service. Tim Conway, his commanding officer, was to say to him, "For conduct unbecoming an officer, you are to be expelled from military service." With that one sentence, he would then begin to tear off Harvey's insignias. The fun of the sketch came when Harvey's insignias would not come off. His buttons could not be ripped from his uniform. However, Tim would then test it on his own uniform and his insignias, buttons, brass, and everything else came off easily. The end result was Harvey standing at attention perfectly dressed while Tim was in his underwear.

During that sketch, Harvey had only to stand at perfect attention. He had no words to speak, no actions to perform. He simply had to stand at attention.

So, at the taping, Tim went into a wacky discourse on why he was being drummed out of the corps. It went on and on and got wackier and crazier and poor Harvey could do nothing but try to stifle the laughter.

The laughter was always real, though, because Carol would not permit any phoniness on the show; that would be too transparent. If something goofy happened, that was fine. The cast could go with it. However, it could never be written in as a planned flub. That was verboten.

A big part of the show's success was Carol Burnett's opening talk with the audience. It established her as a real person, warm and friendly. From that basis sprang all the goofiness on the show. Again, Carol was fiercely honest with that segment. The questions were never planted and Carol never had pre-arranged responses . . . except once.

In a moment of weakness, Carol allowed one of the writers to be a plant. It was a phony question with a planned bit to accompany it. It was a mistake. It worked horribly because the audience saw through it. Carol vowed after that, to never allow anything phony on the show.

The list of guests on *The Carol Burnett Show* read like a Who's Who of Hollywood and television. It seemed like everyone appeared on the show sooner or later. We used to do a take-off of *Sunset Boulevard* with Carol playing the Gloria Swanson part. She played it absolutely wacky. Nevertheless, Gloria Swanson wrote and suggested that they have the original Norma Desmond on the show.

We booked her. She was about ninety-years-old when she was a guest on the show and she did a dance number. She sang and danced. Well, she sang and the guys in the dance line *carried* her around the stage. We kidded the costume department afterwards at how well they did at designing a dress with handles.

One of our guests enjoyed the week of rehearsals and tapings so much that he gave us a gift. Sammy Davis performed his whole night-club act for the cast and crew, hiring the musicians on his own. We weren't really that thrilled with it.

After the Wednesday rehearsal, Joe Hamilton announced that the post-rehearsal writers' meeting was cancelled. Instead, we were all to report to studio 33. On Wednesday after rehearsal, we were happy to get the meeting out of the way, do any rewrites that need to be done, stop for an after-work cocktail, and then get on home.

When we got to studio 33, we looked at a bare stage. Then, a few musicians walked onstage with their instruments and began setting up. Then, a few more. It began to dawn on us that we were going to see a show. We didn't want to see a show. We wanted to go home.

Sammy came out and announced that he had so much fun working with all of us that he would pay us back the only way he knew how. With that, he signaled the orchestra and they began the music for his first number.

Sammy did an hour of singing, dancing, impersonating, and joke telling. Even though we didn't want to be there, it was great entertainment. During the show I leaned over to Carol Burnett and whispered, "This is going to put a lot of pressure on Roddy McDowell." Roddy was our guest for the upcoming week.

Carol used that line when she thanked Sammy Davis after the show. It worked well. When the studio was clearing, Carol rushed over to my partner, Bill Richmond, gave him a hug and a kiss, and thanked him for the wonderful line to end the show.

It was my line, but that happens often with writing partners.

Some of the guests were not too happy with the material. Telly

Savalas was featured in a sketch with Harvey Korman and Tim Conway. It was about three businessmen meeting in a restaurant and discussing a client who had switched from one company to another. However, it was written very cleverly by Gary Belkin so that it sounded like a woman was leaving one lover for another. It was a nice sketch, but Savalas didn't like it. He wanted out of it. Carol Burnett, though, convinced him to keep rehearsing it. She assured him it would play well.

Telly agreed to continue, but wasn't sold on the material. He read the lines reluctantly throughout the rehearsals. When we taped the show, he was still hesitant. He came onstage to nice applause, and then spoke his first line with absolutely no conviction. However, the audience laughed uproariously. It really was a funny sketch.

Telly heard that laughter. He looked out into the audience and his eyes lit up. He was funny. The audience loved his lines. From then on, he played the sketch like the biggest comedy ham in the world. He was getting laughs, and he loved it.

When we were about to open the tenth season of the show, Joe Hamilton and Carol wanted a grand opening. They wanted someone with stature to open the show. It was hard to find someone with more stature than Carol. We got some interest from Jack Benny, one of Carol's comedy idols.

Bill Richmond and I wrote a short two or three-page bit in which Jack Benny would wander onto stage 33 at CBS, and from that starting point, would introduce Carol for her tenth season.

Joe Hamilton called us into his office and said, "Jack loves the piece." That was good news to us. "However," Joe said, "he would like to meet with you guys to discuss some changes."

Joe advised us, "When you meet with Jack Benny, give him anything he asks for. We really want him to open the show."

We met with Jack and his manager, Irving Fein.

Jack said, "I love the piece. It's very clever, very funny."

Our hat sizes got bigger.

Jack said, "However, there are just a few things I'd like to know about it."

We said, "Okay."

He said, "Why do I wander onto the stage?"

We said, "Well, you're in CBS and you're lost."

He said, "But I wouldn't walk onto a lighted stage with an audience."

We said, "Well, maybe you think it's another show and you walk out . . . ."

He said, "I'd always check with a stage manager even if I was booked on another show."

Whatever reason we'd offer, Jack would counter with a reason why it wasn't valid.

Finally Irving Fein said, "Look, Jack, it's only a two-minute bit. Why don't you just do it as written?"

Jack said, "How many times do I have to tell you, Irving? When I'm doing a joke about my Stradivarius, *I have to be holding my Stradivarius.*"

Jack never did the show and Bill and I got kidded for the next few weeks as the guys who talked Jack Benny out of being our opening act.

There were some sour points during the five years we worked on the Burnett staff. They were normal; there were always disagreements over jokes and which sketches by which writers were picked for which performers. Overall, though, it was a great, five-year assignment. We wrote some terrific material and had lots of fun. We also collected a few Emmy Awards for our efforts. In five years, the staff was nominated six times. Once, we had two different staffs in one season and both were nominated. We won three of those Emmy Awards.

Chapter Fourteen
The Emmy Awards

The first thought that popped into my head when they handed me the Emmy onstage at the Pantages Theatre was, *"Boy, this thing is heavier than I thought."* The second thought, though, as I held the statue and faced the black-tie audience was, *"This is the peak. After all the hard work I've done building a comedy writing career, this is the seal of approval."* The Emmy was awarded not just to me, of course, but to a team of writers—Gary Belkin, Roger Beatty, Arnie Kogen, Bill Richmond, Rudy DeLuca and Barry Levinson, Dick Clair and Jenna McMahon, and Barry Harman. Still, it was a symbol that I was part of the best writing team of the 1973-1974 television seasons.

There was no pressure to attend the awards show that season, either. We knew we had won. It had never happened before and it probably wouldn't happen again. For some reason, the Academy of Television Arts and Sciences changed their format that year. Our writing staff was notified that the show that had been broadcast on February 16, 1974 had been nominated for an Emmy. Later, the Academy announced that only one writing Emmy would be awarded for the best overall writing of the season. It could be for a variety show or a sitcom, it didn't matter. Only one writer or writing team would win the Emmy.

All other winners in the various categories would not receive statues and would be considered merely as nominees—losing nominees..

The industry wasn't pleased with that format. Performers, including Carol Burnett, announced that they would not attend the show if that system prevailed. The Academy relented and announced that all nominees in the various categories would receive Emmys. Then, there would be an overall winner, who would receive an additional Emmy.

Since we were already the nominee in the Comedy-Variety or Music Series category, we knew we would be awarded a statue.

We didn't win the overall category, though, and that unusual format was dropped after that season.

When the winners walk onstage, someone hands each one an Emmy to hold. As they walk offstage, someone takes it away from them. Then backstage, they run the gantlet of press rooms. Each network news department has a room where the winners stand on a makeshift stage and answers questions. There are several rooms for the newspaper reporters, also. As the winners walk into each of those rooms, someone hands each an Emmy. As they leave, someone takes it away from them.

Of course, the writers were marched through those rooms expeditiously because the press wanted famous faces, not behind-the-scenes writers. We were treated courteously, for the most part, but dismissed quickly. Writers didn't generate much interest.

We left the auditorium without our Emmys. The Academy had to have all the statues engraved with the winners' names and details. They couldn't do it beforehand since they supposedly didn't know who the winners were.

We all tried to be blasé about the win. Ed Simmons, in his acceptance remarks, stated that the real reward for our year of work was not the Emmy, but the privilege of working with Carol Burnett. It was a nice sentiment, but not really true. We were all thrilled with the Emmy.

Our false blasé attitude was exposed when the Academy finally called to tell us that the statuettes were available to be picked up at the Writers Guild offices. All of us skipped lunch to go get our awards.

We walked into a room full of typists. One of them stopped typing long enough to ask how she could help us. We told her we were there to pick up our Emmys. She asked our names and told each of us our assigned number. Then, she directed us to a room in the back of the suite of offices.

That room was a small office with hundreds of Emmy statues wrapped in newspapers like supermarket fish. Each had a small piece of masking tape with a number written on it. The Emmys were on desks, under desks, on shelves, and in drawers, in no particular order. We began our hunt.

"Is anybody number 237?"

"I have 135. Is that anybody?"

"I'm 147. Holler if you see that number."

Finally, after climbing over the desks and shimmying along the floor, we all located our paper-wrapped statues. As we went to leave, the typists ignored us and concentrated on their keyboard tasks.

Bill Richmond couldn't let it go at that. He climbed on top of one desk, straddled the young lady's typewriter, held his newspaper-covered trophy aloft, and announced, "I'd like to thank all the little people . . . ."

The Carol Burnett Show writing staff accepting their first Emmy Award in 1974. L. to R. (back row" Barry Harman, Bill Richmond, Barry Levinson, Arnie Kogen, Dick Clair, Roger Beatty. (front row) Gene Perret, Ed Simmons, Jenna McMahon, Gary Belkin, Rudy DeLuca.

It got a nice laugh.

Back at the Burnett offices, we unwrapped our statues and admired them. I read the plaque at the bottom of my Emmy and noticed that the word "writers" was misspelled. The engraving read, "wri ers." I told the group, "This is wild. On my plaque there's no 't' in the word 'writers.'" Bill Richmond said, "Really? Both 't's' are there on mine."

He was kidding, of course, but I wasn't. I still cherish my misspelled Emmy statuette.

We repeated in 1974-1975 with most of the same team of writers, with the exception of Barry Harman, who had moved on to other projects.

The previous year, when we came onstage at the Emmy Awards, the camera had a close-up of me only once. While it was on me, I covered my face with my hand, but during the awards for 1974-1975, it looked like I had bribed the cameraman. No matter which camera they used to shoot our group, I was facing it. I made up for the camera time that I missed that first year.

The third season of our administration was also the year that *Saturday Night Live* premiered. It was an innovative show that generated a lot of attention and won the writing award for Variety.

They won the following year, too.

We bounced back, though, at the 1977-78 awards telecast. Our writing staff captured the Emmy on the last season of *The Carol Burnett Show*. The staff that year consisted of Ed Simmons, Roger Beatty, Rick Hawkins, Liz Sage, Robert Illes, James Stein, Franelle Silver,

The Carol Burnett Show **writing staff accepting their third Emmy award in 1978. L. to R. (back row) Roger Beatty, Rick Hawkins, Jenna McMahon, Bill Richmond, James, Stein. (front row) Dick Clair, Larry Siegel, Franelle Silver, Robert Illes, Gene Perret, Liz Sage, Ed Simmons.**

Larry Siegel, Tim Conway, Dick Clair, Jenna McMahon, Bill Richmond, and I. Barry Harman, who had left our staff after the first season also captured an Emmy this year for writing an episode of *All in the Family*.

That awards show was telecast from the Civic Auditorium in Pasadena. Ed Simmons and his wife, Bobbi, rented a limousine for the affair and came to our house, near the Civic Auditorium, to dress. My wife, Joanne, and I rode to the affair with them in the limo.

My kids and their friends all rode to the auditorium on their bikes and got right up front. When our limo arrived, all of our kids and their friends cheered like crazy when we got out of our limo. Hearing that uproar, everyone else cheered like crazy, too. They didn't know who we were, but they knew that we must have been somebody special if that many youngsters knew us. Someone in the crowd finally asked, "Who is that?"

My daughter proudly said, "That's my daddy."

The cheering stopped.

Unlike the first year we were nominated, we had no idea whether we would win or not. However, Ed and I told our wives, "If we win, we won't be back in the audience." We wanted them to allow us some time to go through the press rooms, have a backstage drink, and then meet the ladies outside, get our limo, and go to a nearby restaurant, The Chronicle, for dinner.

We won and we met them outside, as planned.

We asked the attendant to call our limo from the parking garage, and he did. No limo arrived. We asked him to call again. He did. No limo arrived. He called again, but there was no response. He sent someone to check on our limo.

Our limo and our limo driver had disappeared. We figured the driver took one look at us, decided we didn't have a chance of winning, so he took the limousine and went to visit his girlfriend or something like that. We don't know what happened, but we took a cab to the restaurant and never saw the limousine again.

Chapter Fifteen
Writing Sitcom Episodes

Television can be an insecure business. I had studied and worked hard to become a solid, one-line writer. Then, I had to learn the craft of sketch writing. Both of those skills served me well in establishing myself as an accomplished variety show writer. Then, variety shows began to disappear from the tube.

On my first year in television, there were fourteen musical-variety shows on the air: *The Andy Williams Show*, *The Carol Burnett Show*, *The Dean Martin Show*, *The Ed Sullivan Show*, *Glen Campbell's Goodtime Hour*, *The Hollywood Palace*, *The Jackie Gleason Show*, *Jimmy Durante Presents the Lennon Sisters Hour*, *The Kraft Music Hall*, *Laugh-In*, *The Leslie Uggams Show*, *The Red Skelton Show*, *This Is Tom Jones*, and the one I worked on, *The Jim Nabors Hour*. That meant that at least 140 comedy writers had employment.

In 1978 on the last year of *The Carol Burnett Show*, there were just three other variety shows on the air: *Donny and Marie*, *The Red Foxx Comedy Hour*, and *The Richard Pryor Show*. That's a lot of gag-writers looking for work.

Bill Richmond and I had become an official writing team while working on *The Carol Burnett Show*. We decided that it would be wise to begin to build credits in sitcom writing so that we'd have some credibility when Burnett went off the air.

We began promoting ourselves for story sessions and we had good luck. The producing team of Bernie Kukoff and Jeff Harris were looking for stories for their show, *Joe and Sons*, starring Richard Castellano. We pitched them a tale about the young kid, the "Son" of *Joe and Sons*, minding a plant for his friend who was going on vacation. The friend treated the plant like a pet, but when Joe saw it in the house, he mistook it for marijuana. That was the basic plot. The producers bought it and gave us the assignment.

We began to learn the idiosyncrasies of sitcom writing and dealing with producers and networks. In our first draft, we had Joe take one tiny leaf from the plant and taste it, supposedly testing to see if it was contraband or not. The producers objected. "The friend treats this plant like a beloved pet," they said. "We can't mutilate it that way."

We thought that was a bit silly, but it was their game, so we played by their rules. We rewrote the script and deleted the part where Joe tore off one tiny leaf.

We got paid for our work, and then we went back to our work on *The Carol Burnett Show*. When our *Joe and Sons* episode aired, we were stunned. Jerry Stiller co-starred on the show as Joe's best friend. After the in-house rewrite that was approved by the same producers, Jerry Stiller was holding the beloved plant when a policeman came to the door regarding another matter. The Stiller character panicked and ate the entire plant . . . the *entire plant.*

We did land a second assignment with *Joe and Sons*. I forget the basic premise, but after writing most of the script, we were stuck for an ending. We had sort of painted ourselves into a corner and were having trouble resolving the plot.

One evening, when the Burnett workday ended, Bill and I resolved to stay at the office and finalize the last few pages of that *Joe and Sons* script. We wanted to end it, get it sent off to Kukoff and Harris, and get paid. We also wanted to find out how the story ended. Until then, we had no idea.

So we put away our work on *The Carol Burnett Show*, and put a blank page into the typewriter. Almost as soon as the page was positioned, we got a call from Kukoff and Harris. "Put whatever you've got into an envelope and get it to us immediately," they said.

"But it's not finished," we told them.

"That's all right. We've been cancelled. Get us whatever pages you have and we'll issue you a check in payment."

We sent the unfinished manuscript up to their office and will never know how the story ended.

It did end in a paycheck, though.

Mort Lochman, a former Bob Hope writer-producer, was producing *All in the Family*. Their offices were down the corridor from our Burnett cubicles. We passed in the hallways often. Mort asked Bill Richmond and I to come up with some stories for *All in the Family*.

We agreed to a pitch session and spent an afternoon and an evening working on possible story lines. When we had about five or six that we felt we could write, we called and set up an appointment with Mort.

We came up with another devious scheme, though. We wrote each of the premises on a single index card and planted them in different pockets. At the pitch session with Mort and Milt Josefsberg, another former Hope writer, we started verbalizing our story lines. The first concerned the birthday of Archie Bunker's grandson. We had Archie buying the youngster a toy gun. Meathead, Archie's son-in-law and the kid's father, objected to that. He had bought the young boy a doll. The basic conflict was about whether or not the kid should have a manly toy like a gun or a sissy toy like a doll.

Mort and Milt were intrigued by that tale and seemed inclined to buy it. However, like all good producers, they said, "What else have you got?"

We said, "That's it."

They said, "You come to a pitch session with only one story?"

We said, "Yeah."

Then, we took the index card out of our pocket and showed it to them. It had only the one story line written on it.

They said, "You guys have courage, but we'll buy it."

We got the sale.

If we had gone in with the other story lines we had conceived, they probably would have been torn. "Do I like the first story or the third one? Of course, that last one you pitched wasn't bad, either." They would have wavered back and forth among several of them and the meeting might have ended with them wanting to mull it over. We would have left with no sale and chances were that they would have never made a decision nor called with a final sale.

We wrote the story about the birthday and the toy gun versus the doll. They probably had some notes and we did a rewrite. Mort loved the script. Each time we passed in the corridor after that, he said, "You guys gotta come up with a new script for us."

It just so happened that we were tied up on Carol Burnett's show and couldn't find the time to come up with a new script. We kept putting him off.

Nevertheless, he kept asking. "When are you guys coming in for another story meeting?"

Then we watched the episode of *All in the Family* that we had written, only to find that *one line in the script was ours.*

The next time Mort asked us for a new script, we said, "Just use the one we gave you before."

It was neither uncommon nor illogical for a producer to love a script so much and yet change every line of it before taping. Stories have a certain feel, and that was what Mort liked about our script. The story worked. However, a script went through many changes from first draft to taping. It was read by all the performers and they made notes and offered suggestions. They slightly changed lines to suit their speech patterns, and some wanted a certain joke improved or changed. Then, they had a table reading and many people offered notes and suggestions. During rehearsals, stage business was altered and lines were changed. All those changes were gradual and didn't really change the story. Yet, when the script was finalized, it was totally different from the original. So, it is conceivable that they would have liked our work and yet changed it drastically.

All those adventures were diversions. Our main work was on *The Carol Burnett Show.*" The episodic writing we did was an investment in our future. It was almost a sideline for us. We knew that the Burnett show would end and we'd be thrust into sitcom work in earnest. We learned there were many more heartbreaks when we worked on it full time.

Chapter Sixteen
Welcome Back, Kotter

After Carol Burnett retired her show, we were out of work. It didn't take long to get our next assignment, though. Bill Richmond and I agreed to produce *Welcome Back, Kotter*. Ed Simmons was influential in landing us the job. Ed was hired as the new executive producer of the show. Well, he wasn't really the executive producer because Jimmy Komack, who originated the show, held that title, and he wasn't the producer because Ed insisted that Bill and I be brought on as producers. Ed was in limbo. He asked the Writers Guild if he could simply list himself as "Boss" on the credits. They refused. To this day, I don't know what title he finally wound up with. It must be on the credits.

Rick Hawkins and Liz Sage also came along with Ed, Bill, and I from *The Carol Burnett Show*.

It seemed like the ideal job because the show was relatively successful and we had a nucleus of writers that we knew, liked, and had worked with before. After about five weeks on the job, we all resigned.

There had been problems on the show in previous seasons. Gabe Kaplan, the star of the show, didn't care for Jimmy Komack. Marcia Strassman, who played Mrs. Kotter on the sitcom, didn't get along with Gabe. Komack wasn't crazy about Kaplan. There were several feuds going on. However, our writing and producing staff honestly came onto the show with an open mind. We wanted to write well and make the show even better than it was before. We weren't aware of the specifics of the feuds and we didn't want to know the details. We wanted to deal with everyone as fairly as we could and not take sides.

Jimmy Komack was pretty above board when we came onto the show. He didn't bad mouth anyone and didn't share any of his likes or dislikes with us. He treated us simply as writers and producers. Fair enough.

Gabe didn't have the same attitude. He assumed that because Komack hired us, we were on Komack's side. He was wrong, but it never stopped him from acting on his belief.

We first met Gabe at the Brown Derby in Beverly Hills. Komack scheduled a luncheon meeting with Gabe, Ed Simmons, Bill Richmond, and I. It was a "get acquainted—let's find out where we all stand" kind of luncheon. Since Jimmy, Ed, Bill, and I worked in the same office, we went to the luncheon meeting together. Gabe arrived later and alone. The first thing he said as he sat down was, "You used my name on the reservation to get a better table, huh?"

I suppose whoever made the reservation did, but it's still an arrogant way to greet the new staff. Gabe was petulant from the beginning. I don't remember anything of substance coming out of that meeting because Kaplan didn't want to hear it. He had his feud. In his mind, he knew we were Komack's lackeys. He wanted to be irritated.

When we got into production, he became even more troublesome. We wrote the shows, rewrote them, rehearsed them for a few days, and then Gabe showed up on Wednesday (sometimes Thursday) and found fault with everything—the premise, the plot, the scenes, and the individual jokes. We had no objection to him voicing his opinions. It was basically his show and he was the one who had to stand on camera and recite the lines. He was entitled to request changes.

Our objection was with the timing of Gabe's complaints. It took time to make changes, especially basic alterations to the story line. We didn't mind changing a few lines of dialogue, adding a new and better joke, or even rewriting portions of scenes. All television writers are used to working late into the night and coming up with new dialogue and funnier jokes. We even put in late hours making considerable scene changes, but it was totally unreasonable to ask for a major rewrite starting with plot point number one just one or two days before the taping. Good writing can't be done that quickly, nor can the cast rehearse the new teleplay well enough to give a credible performance on tape day.

Besides, it was apparent that Gabe was demanding those changes just to be disagreeable. If he really felt that strongly about the show and each individual taping, he should have been available to work with the writers (or against them, as the case may be) as the original story was being conceived. His input would have been somewhat welcome and more tolerable at conception, rather than hours before the taping.

So for several weeks, Kaplan kept complaining about the scripts and demanding changes well after those changes could reasonably have been made. When we refused to make most of his changes, he considered that to be further proof that we hated him, were siding with Komack, and were being recalcitrant just to get revenge against him. It wasn't true. The radical changes he demanded simply couldn't be made in such a short time.

That situation caused our creative staff considerable distress. First of all, we did have to make many of the changes that he wanted. We were trying to be reasonable, and a certain amount of revisions were expected. Secondly, it was a constant battle. Everything we did was unacceptable to Gabe Kaplan.

One morning, our *Carol Burnett Show* nucleus was sitting in Ed Simmons's office schmoozing before the work day started. Ed happened to mention that he had an uneasy feeling in his stomach. It was probably the stress of producing that show each week against Kaplan's complaints. Bill said he felt the same way, and so did Rick, Liz, and I.

Ed Simmons said, "Why are we doing this?"

With that, we all marched into Jimmy Komack's office and asked to be let out of our contracts.

Jimmy asked us to hold off until he could call a meeting with David Wolper, who had a financial interest in the show. We agreed.

Before we got into the details of the meeting, though, it was important to note that we had scored some important points as the new writing-producing staff on the show.

John Travolta, who was on the show from its beginning as one of the Sweathogs, was probably the biggest movie star in Hollywood at that time. His films *Saturday Night Fever* and *Grease* were huge successes and John was the current reigning movie idol. He didn't need *Welcome Back, Kotter* any longer. He didn't want to do the show with all the bickering. He had enough money and movie offers to keep him busy without a weekly series.

Jimmy Komack asked John Travolta to meet with Ed Simmons, and Bill and I—the new season's production team. Travolta agreed and we all piled into a limousine to meet at John's rented house in Malibu where he was making a film with Lily Tomlin.

We told him our plans for the show. He asked questions about how we would handle certain aspects of the show. We talked about *Welcome Back, Kotter* for a couple of hours.

At the end of the meeting, John said he would do seven to ten shows for us during the coming season. Getting him on board was a feather in our producing hats.

As for what we were to do about Gabe Kaplan, at a meeting with Komack and Wolper, we explained why we were unsatisfied with the working of the show. Gabe was throwing monkey wrenches into the works weekly. We didn't feel we could produce the show that way and we felt that we didn't have to. We'd just as soon leave as continue the way things were going.

David Wolper asked what it would take for us to stay.

We said, "Get rid of Gabe Kaplan."

It was kind of a daring stand, to ask a show to dump the star because we weren't happy. However, we felt that strongly about the problems he was causing us and the show.

Wolper and Komack suggested keeping Gabe for maybe seven to ten shows, just like Travolta. We said no.

They suggested having him in three or four shows. Again, we refused. We wanted him gone.

Finally, we arrived at a compromise. Gabe Kaplan, as Mr. Kotter, would open and close each show by telling a joke to his wife played by Marcia Strassman. That would be the opening and the closing of the show—the teaser and the *tag*. That's all Kaplan would do on the show. He would not be involved in the teleplay itself and he would not be involved in the writing or rewriting of the teleplay. We stayed under those conditions.

Then we had another problem. David Wolper was not happy with the script that Bill and I had written for John Travolta's first appearance on the show. Because John would only be involved in selected shows, we wanted to separate him from the rest of the Sweathogs in a positive way. Also, we had to explain his absence from the shows that he wouldn't be appearing in. We had Vinnie Barbarino, John's character on the show, leave school and get a job.

Wolper hated that idea and he told us so in the most profane language you can imagine. As writers, we had heard most of the bad words going around at the time, but we had never her words spoken so fiercely or frequently. He was furious.

David Wolper wanted us to feature John Travolta with the Dallas Cowboy Cheerleaders. He wanted to turn the show into a Hollywood extravaganza with girls and glitz and anything else we could add to get ratings. We felt that was wrong and told him so when we got a chance to talk. Eventually, we did the show we wanted to do, but David Wolper was never happy about it.

Gabe wasn't happy, either, but we didn't care. Even though he was no longer involved in the show's story lines, he still gave us problems even when he was doing only the opening and closing gag on each show.

We would tape Gabe's pieces before we got into taping the actual teleplay each week. That way, we could get him on tape and dismiss him. It made our lives easier.

At one taping, Gabe wasn't happy with the gag he had. In front of the studio audience he screamed out, "Where are the writers? Do any of you have a better joke?"

We all screamed back in unison, "No."

Gabe did the joke as written and left.

Of course, we had other problems during the year with the cast. Individual cast members have complaints during the season.

"I'm not getting enough to do on the show"

"How come she has more lines than I have?"

Some of the complaints were common and predictable, but others surprised us. Most, though, were the kind of problems producers dealt with while producing any show.

The biggest irritant to me was when the actors playing Sweathogs all wanted a funny line anytime anyone else had a funny line. Each came into our office.

"You know when Bobby says that line that gets the big laugh?"

We'd say, "Yes."

"Well, I think I should say something there."

Then, another actor playing a Sweathog came in.

"If he's going to say something after Bobby's big laugh, I think I should have something funny to say."

The show started to take on an unnatural feel. No matter who said what, they were always followed by two or three other people commenting on the same thing. It was unwieldy, and none of them was satisfied having another get a laugh without them having a topper.

I used to try to tell them about Jack Benny. He was most generous in giving the laugh lines to the supporting performers because it made the show funnier. At the end of the show, it still read *The Jack*

Benny Show. By letting others get big laughs, he shared in the glory. The show was funny and that's what mattered.

Not to our cast, though.

We should have known we were in for problems like that when we met the first cast member. We were all working in pre-production, getting shows ready for taping. The cast had not been called to work yet.

Ron Palillo, who played Horshack on the show, stopped in at the offices one morning to meet the new production staff. He had been doing a Neil Simon play in San Francisco during the hiatus. He told us about it. "Yeah, I was doing Neil Simon. I changed a lot of the lines and made them funnier. It was great."

When an actor starts rewriting America's greatest comedy playwright, you know the writing staff is in for some headaches.

We had a problem, too, when John Travolta came in to do his first show. By then, John had an entourage and was assigned a larger dressing room than the other cast members. Also, because there were so many youngsters eager to be there to see John, we had to have extra security around the studio.

One by one, the other actors came in to complain about that. Their contracts called for equal treatment all around, so they asked why Travolta was getting a larger dressing room. We tried to explain that he needed the extra room because he was also working on movies and others were working in his dressing area. I'm not sure they bought that, but they couldn't do much about it except complain.

Then, Bobby Hegyes, who played Epstein on the show, complained that John was getting more security than he was. I said, "Bobby, I'll walk you home tonight."

It didn't make him any happier.

Sometimes we caused ourselves our own headaches, too.

Marcia Strassman requested a meeting with Bill Richmond and me and complained that she had nothing to do on the shows and that none of the plays revolved around her. We listened and tried to be fair. She did have a valid grievance, after all. We searched for and found one upcoming show that could be retooled and made to feature Mrs. Kotter, Marcia's character.

We discussed what changes we would make with her. She seemed satisfied and we got to work redoing some of the scripts. We took Marcia out of one show where she felt she wasn't being utilized adequately. Then we rewrote another show making her the central character.

Problem solved. Everyone was happy again.

The following Monday, we were preparing to begin the table reading for that week's show.   We waited for the entire cast to show up. Marcia wasn't there. We waited some more. Finally, I called her and told her in no uncertain terms that she'd better be there within the next half hour.

I came back and told my partner what I had done. Our secretary overheard my comments, called me aside, and said, "This is the show that you wrote Marcia out of. She doesn't have to be here today."

Oh boy.

I went down to the entrance gate which was just outside our offices at ABC. Marcia drove her convertible through the gate at an angry speed. I signaled for her. She squealed to a stop next to me. Very apologetically, I said, "Marcia, I didn't realize that you were not in this week's . . . ."

She hit the gas, did a U-turn like a stunt driver, and burned rubber right out of the gate again.

I don't think she accepted my apology, and I don't think she talked to me much for the rest of the season.

There have been documentaries discussing who caused the downfall of *Welcome Back, Kotter*. Gabe Kaplan and some of the other performers apparently felt that it was the joke-writing squad from *The Carol Burnett Show,* who couldn't handle situation comedy writing. Some feel it was the infighting on the show that hurt it.

The truth is that it was never a very strong show; it was never a real show. It was a farce. Those Sweathogs were from a poor neighborhood and poor families, yet when they wanted to do a hospital sketch, they got gurneys, doctor's outfits, stethoscopes, and whatever they needed.

We were as guilty as the other staffs. In one show, we had Ron Palillo take his first alcoholic drink, become a raging alcoholic, see the error of his ways, and cure himself of his addiction, all in the space of about twenty-three minutes of airtime. It was silly.

In an effort to replace John Travolta, we brought in Stephen Shortridge, a male model. His character never caught on.

To boost sagging ratings, we even had Ron Palillo get engaged and married. We thought an on-screen wedding would pull ratings. It didn't help. Nothing helped.

The show was in its fourth year when we inherited it. The ratings were declining and it was very difficult to reverse a downward trend in television. We couldn't do it. At the end of our administration, *Welcome Back, Kotter* was cancelled. The writing-producing staff, though, fared better than the performers. We all moved on to another show the following season. It took some of them a little longer.

Chapter Seventeen
Three's Company

Three's Company was the only show I ever signed on with while at sea. Despite being out of work after the cancellation of *Welcome Back, Kotter,* my wife and I went on a cruise to Mexico. We relaxed and enjoyed the cruise, while my agent was busy trying to get me employed for the upcoming season.

He was successful at finding work for our writing team. He called me while we were floating somewhere in the Pacific and said, "I've got an offer for you guys to produce *Three's Company.*

I said, "I hate that show."

He said, "Make it better."

I really did dislike *Three's Company.* It was a popular show, sometimes finishing as the #1 show in the ratings. To me, though, it was cheap, immature humor that was badly written.

I wanted to think about it. My agent emphasized that we didn't have much time to decide. The show needed an answer soon, or they'd look elsewhere.

I tried to call Bill Richmond—not a fast or easy process from sea. When I reached him, he was as unsure as I was. He didn't care much for the show, either.

My agent called back later and I was still not sold on the project.

He impressed on me, though, that it was a top-rated show, and more importantly, it was employment and a nice salary. Finally, I agreed to go along with whatever Bill Richmond wanted to do. Since he was more available than I was for back and forth negotiations, I let him make the decisions for the team.

Later, my agent left word that Bill and I were indeed the new producers of *Three's Company*.

Three's Company was run by the team of Don Nicholl, Mickey Ross, and Bernie West – NRW. They'd spent several years before producing *All in the Family*. I had gone to a pitch session with them when they were producing that show and apparently neither my story ideas nor I impressed them. I didn't get a sale then, but now I was working as a producer under them as executive producers.

When Bill and I first reported to work, only Don Nicholl and Bernie West were on the job. Mickey had been vacationing in Europe when his wife took seriously ill. He stayed on with her until she was well enough to journey back to California.

We started off well. The writing staff was already in place when we were hired to produce, so we had no input on who would be writing the show. Nevertheless, we got on well with the writers. Don and Bernie welcomed us onto the show and all seemed to be going pleasantly.

Sometime during the first week or so while we were producers, NRW's secretary came over to give us some of the ground rules of the show. Apparently, NRW had strict regulations and we were to know them and abide by them.

First, there was to be no green clothing worn on tape day. I supposed this was some sort of British show business tradition that they subscribed to. That was no real problem, but when things started to turn sour, I snuck into tape day wearing green underwear . . . strictly for spite.

Second, when the Holy Trinity was in their office playing darts, which they did often, they were not to be disturbed by anyone for any reason. I thought that with the pressures of running a show, that was childish and unreasonable, but it was their show. We tried to abide by it for as long as we could. However, I felt, if a serious problem came up that needed their attention, I'd interrupt no matter who was winning the dart game.

Third, we were not to attend the note session following the Wednesday rehearsal. That was a sacred time for the Triumvirate, NRW, and the cast. They wanted no outside interference. We producers, it seemed, were considered "outsiders." However, it was their show, so we'd adhere to that restriction, too. That instruction proved to be an important factor later in the season.

As I mentioned earlier, I always thought the show was badly written. It was slapstick, sophomoric, cheap, and bent any rules of structure for an easy laugh. Here are a few examples:

In one show, for whatever reason, Jack, played by John Ritter, was hiding from the authorities. When the police came to the apartment, Chrissy, played by Suzanne Somers, pretended she was taking a shower, and Jack hid behind the curtains with her. The police came into the bathroom, but quickly retreated when they thought Chrissy was naked behind the curtains. They left. However, one of the policemen had left his hat in the bathroom. He went back and simply opened the door to retrieve his hat, of course, forcing Jack and Chrissy into some laughable shenanigans to try to cover up again. To me, no policeman would barge back into a bathroom like that without either announcing it or knocking. It bent reality to get the easy laughs.

Another example was when Jack, for some reason, was masquerading as a woman—again, to escape the law. You can see from those plots why I felt the way I did about the show's writing. Throughout the half-hour, Jack disguised himself as a female. At the show's end, he dramatically tore off his wig and revealed that he was really a man. The problem was that John Ritter's hair at that time was as long as most females. He looked as much like a woman with the wig off as he did with it on.

Bad writing.

Nevertheless, the show was as well-run and as well-organized as any on television at that time. NRW ran a tight ship.

First, they totally ignored the network executives, their demands, and their requests. As far as Nicholl, Ross, and West were concerned, they handled the show. The network simply gave them money and airtime. It wasn't a bad way to produce a show.

On *Welcome Back, Kotter,* for example, we had to submit every story idea to the network executive in charge. He either approved or rejected that particular story idea before we began writing it. That not only limited creativity, but it was also time-consuming. Time was paramount in producing a weekly half-hour sitcom. On *Three's Company,* we told the network nothing. The executives weren't even permitted at the readings or the rehearsals. According to NRW, they didn't exist. That was fine with Bill and me.

Second, NRW controlled the cast and the performers. Richard Klein played Larry, a neighbor, on the show. The character, Larry, had no last name. Richard always asked for a last name. As an actor, he felt it gave his character more depth. The Triumvirate never gave him one. It was their way of keeping actors subservient to them. It was petty, I suppose, but it was their way.

Once, Bill Richmond complimented one of the actors on the performance or on some piece of business he added to the script. Don Nicholl talked to both Bill and I afterwards and admonished us never to compliment the actors. If we built up their egos or their self-esteem, he felt, we made them harder to handle and harder to manipulate.

Third, NRW controlled the scripts. They rewrote, refined, and polished every script right before it went for printing and distribution to the cast. Every plot point, every joke, every line of dialogue had to meet with their approval. If it didn't, they changed it.

Again, I felt the show was poorly written and they were the reason for that, but the show was badly written consistently. That was a good thing. Good or bad, the show had an imprint. It was NRW.

The Triumvirate was totally in charge of all aspects of the show, and that was beneficial. Most of the good shows throughout television history have been those which had strong leadership. With one person, or one entity in charge, the show was more organized.

NRW's leadership was commendable.

We survived well under NW, but the troubles began when R came back onto the show. R, of course, being Mickey Ross – the R in NRW. Almost immediately Mickey began to sabotage Bill and me.

When he first arrived back in the states and into the offices, he came over to introduce himself and to welcome us as the new producers of Three's Company. He sat in our office and chatted with us quite amiably, telling us how good a writer he was and that he was a genius.

He told us that when he thought about plot points in a script, he could literally stop his watch. He was serious. I wasn't.

I said, "It's a pity to waste that talent on a show like *Three's Company*." I told him, "You should either get a better show or a better watch."

Come to think of it, maybe Mickey did have a good reason to dislike us.

I could only guess why Mickey was so disruptive to our producing and head writing efforts. Perhaps he just didn't like us. It could be that he didn't like our writing. He might have been upset that we had been hired without his input. Possibly we were doing such a good job that he felt threatened by us. Who knows?

Mickey was strange even within a strange triumvirate. Don was the most rational of the three and the dominant one. He was the boss. Mickey was the congenital egotist. He not only thought he knew everything about comedy, but that he was the only one who knew anything about comedy. As far as I was concerned, he was way off base on both counts. Bernie was the whipping boy of the three. He was the one that the other two bullies ridiculed.

At one meeting, several writers were trying to solve a script problem along with Bernie West and Mickey Ross. Bernie suddenly stood up and claimed to have the solution. He walked around the room adlibbing plot points and jokes. After about five minutes of his dissertation, he ended, turned to Mickey and said, "What do you think?"

Mickey said, "I'm sorry, Bernie, I wasn't listening."

Mickey apparently was absorbed trying to stop his watch and couldn't pay any attention to his partner.

The incident left a foul taste in my mouth.

After Mickey had been back in the office for a couple of weeks, NRW called a meeting, probably at Mickey's prompting because he did most of the talking at the session.

Nicholl, Ross, and West were at the meeting, along with Bill and I, and all of the writing staff. Mickey began with, "We have a serious problem with upcoming scripts."

That was the first Bill and I knew of any crisis, so we asked what it was.

Mickey said, "We don't have enough stories lined up."

That came as a shock to us because we had turned in several stories for NRW's approval. I told them that. "We have several ideas in your office, but we can't get an answer from you on them."

Mickey ignored that statement. He continued to berate the staff for not being industrious enough. Again, I mentioned that if we got approval on the script ideas we'd already submitted, we could get to work on the scripts.

Again, he ignored the statement.

We didn't necessarily want approval of the ideas, but if they weren't satisfactory, let us know so that the writing team could come up with alternatives.

NRW insisted on treating those ideas as if they didn't exist at all.

The entire session was an affront to Bill and I as producers, first because NRW didn't initially discuss it with us. We were responsible for the scripts. If they weren't happy with the ideas or with the number of ideas, they should have come to us so that we could correct the situation. They didn't. That meeting was the first we knew of any dissatisfaction.

Second, they discussed the problem in front of the entire writing staff. That undercut our credibility tremendously. We were not only reduced to just being a part of the writing staff, but we were the ones being held up as responsible for the problem. In other words, they took away our authority, yet used that same authority to blame us for the problem.

We weren't happy with that meeting.

Third, the meeting was a sham. There was no problem. We had submitted plenty of stories. We had enough scripts on paper to keep us in production for several weeks, and we had enough story lines suggested to keep the writers working to get those scripts completed in plenty of time. The entire agenda of that meeting was manufactured by Mickey to humiliate us.

It did that. It also infuriated Bill and me.

The pleasant part of *Three's Company* was the cast. They respected the writing and were very gracious to Bill and me, the new producers, and they were fun to work with.

John Ritter made it a point to keep everyone enthused and positive, even when there were problems. He and Suzanne Somers were the Martin and Lewis of rehearsals and meetings. They paid attention and did whatever was asked of them, but they also clowned around just enough to keep all the activities light-hearted. Any minor crisis with the script or the rehearsal was solved amidst a good bit of laughter generated by the antics of John and Suzanne.

Joyce DeWitt and Don Knotts were cooperative, pleasant, and quite talented in their roles.

One crisis stands out in my memory, though. It was during the week when Don Knotts was featured as the central character in the script. It was his show.

Normally, we read the new script on Monday morning, took notes, and made changes. Then, we let the cast rehearse it without interference from the writers until Wednesday. On that day, we had a run-through of the entire show with the crew, the writers, the producers, and the executive producers. After that, we had a note session (the one we were told never to attend) and changes were made in the script before the taping on Friday.

Bill and I got a call on Monday to go to the rehearsal hall to settle a problem. When we arrived, Don Knotts greeted us with his complaints. He said, "This is one show that features me and no one is working on it. If things don't get straightened out soon, I'm packing my things and going home."

Bill Richmond tried to lighten things up by saying, "Hey, I'll get my hat and go with you."

That really sent Don Knotts through the roof. "I'm serious," he screamed. "This show is important to me, but nothing's getting done. Everyone's on the phone, or off doing something or other. I want it settled now, or I'm leaving."

He was serious. He was angry. The funny part was that the angrier Don got, the higher pitched his normally high-pitched voice got. It was hard for us to settle down to learning the situation while trying not to laugh at Don's runaway voice.

The problem was that it was Suzanne Somers's birthday. Her husband called to offer congratulations. Her manager had flowers delivered every hour on the hour, which meant messengers with gifts were constantly interrupting the rehearsal. The manager also called every hour so that Suzanne was always being called to the phone. The others didn't want to be playing second fiddle to Suzanne, so they had to manufacture reasons why they were to be called away from the studio. Don had a valid point.

We called the cast together and reasoned with them. Their intent was not to disrupt the rehearsals for Don's teleplay, so once they were aware of the problem, they resolved it themselves.

Most of the incidents with the cast were settled quickly and amiably. Our problems with NRW couldn't.

One time, we were permitted to enter the inner sanctum. Ross and West were both absent from the Wednesday rehearsal and Bill and I were asked to fill in at the note session after the rehearsal (the one we were told never to attend). We did. We gave our opinion on the show we had just seen. We offered solutions for any script problems. Actually, we enjoyed it. Participation like that was what producers should be doing.

After the meeting, most of the cast thanked us for our ideas.

Don Nicholl went out of his way to thank us for being there and for taking such an active role in the proceedings.

Again, we were happy to do it.

We were never invited back to another one. The big, decisive problem happened because of a Los Angeles Rams football game. The Rams were playing an important game on Monday evening and it was blacked out in the Los Angeles area. However, CBS was to show the game on their feed.

I opted to have dinner and then come back to the office to watch the game.

Sometime during the telecast, I went into the conference room where we had a refrigerator with snacks and cold drinks. I thought I was alone in the offices, but I wasn't. Mickey Ross was conducting a meeting in the conference room with the writing staff.

I said, "What the hell is going on?"

Mickey said, "We're going over a few scripts that are in trouble."

I said, "Without the producers and the head-writers?"

Mickey offered some sort of excuse for why it wasn't necessary that we be there.

I said, "Well, you can have all of your meetings without us from now on because as of right now, we quit."

I stormed out.

I went back to my office and called my partner, Bill Richmond. I told him I had just resigned both of us from the show. With no hesitation, Bill said, "Whatever you do, I'm with you."

The following morning, Don Nicholl called us into a meeting in the NRW office. Mickey and Bernie were there, too.

Don said, "What would it take to make you stay?"

I said, "Nothing."

I told Don about the writers meeting behind the producers back and added, "You guys don't need producers. You want to do everything yourself."

We resisted any efforts to keep us on the show.

Then, I suppose once Don realized that we couldn't be swayed, he pointed out some of our flaws. He said, "You guys showed a lack of communication on this show."

I asked how he arrived at that decision.

He said, "Well, for one thing you never came to any of the Wednesday note sessions."

I screamed, "We were emphatically told not to attend."

He said, "By whom?"

I said, "Your secretary."

He said, "My God, don't take orders from her."

I said, "She represented herself as speaking on your behalf."

He said, "That's nonsense."

"Besides," I said, "our office is only twelve steps from your office. If you wanted us at those Wednesday meetings, why didn't you march over to our office and tell us to be there? Isn't that really a lack of communication?"

We cleared out our desks the same day and were gone.

We were signed as producers/head-writers of Tim Conway's upcoming variety show almost before we left.

Chapter Eighteen
The Tim Conway Show

Even after *The Carol Burnett Show* went off the air, Joe Hamilton kept his offices at CBS. They were down the corridor from our *Three's Company* suite. Occasionally, Bill Richmond and I stopped in to say hello and a chat. One time, Tim Conway was visiting, too. Tim hadn't done any regular weekly shows since Carol went off the air.

Joe asked how we were doing on *Three's Company*. At the time, things were going well and I told him so. I especially praised the cast. I said, "John Ritter is probably the best physical comedian in television."

Conway started to cough at that remark. His phony cough was meant to say, "Hey, how about me? I'm a physical comedian, too, you know."

When I got the message, I immediately corrected me statement. I said, "Oh, I'm sorry. I mean John Ritter is probably the best physical comedian *working* in television."

We didn't know it at the time, but Tim and Joe were discussing the chances of getting a Tim Conway variety show on the CBS schedule. They were feeling us out to see if they might lure us away from *Three's Company* to produce and head the writing staff on Tim's new show.

As things turned out, they didn't have to entice us; we were going to quit before the end of the current season anyway. When we did resign from *Three's Company,* we immediately got a generous offer to produce Tim's show, and we took it.

Getting back into variety was like coming home after a long exile. We were coming back to a form of writing that we enjoyed, to a production company where we knew and liked the people we would be working with. We were even coming back to our old offices.

Most of all, we were getting out of sitcom writing. Neither Bill Richmond nor I enjoyed writing sitcoms . . . for several reasons. It meant writing for a limited amount of characters. Even on gang shows like *Welcome Back, Kotter,* there were only so many characters we could write for and only so many different stories that we could do. After a while, the writing, the plots, the jokes became monotonous. In variety, we could create different characters each week. If we liked a certain character, we could reprise it. If we tired of it after several versions, we could retire that character. Each week's writing had a newness to it that was invigorating for the creative staff.

The stories after a sitcom had been on the air for awhile tended to become frivolous. Of course, the sketches in variety are trivial, also, but everyone knows and admits that. In sitcoms, people sometimes felt that the stories were high drama with profound meaning. They weren't. They couldn't be in a half-hour's time.

Once on *Three's Company* we were running down some ideas for possible physical bits in one of the shows. Bill and I suggested that Jack could accidentally slam the front door as he was passing by for whatever reason. Mickey Ross, who thought everything was a dramatic highpoint and that his silly sitcom would outlive Shakespeare's plays, said, "I know this apartment very well. That front door would never do that."

Each character in a sitcom eventually thinks that he or she is the star of the show. On *Welcome Back, Kotter,* for instance, Gabe Kaplan felt that the show centered around Kotter. It didn't. It featured the Sweathogs. However, each Sweathog felt he was the main Sweathog. He wasn't. It was true on every show. Each person in the cast wanted the funniest lines, the smartest come backs, and for the plot to revolve around him or her.

Sooner or later, the actors appropriated their character. "I know what that character would say or do because I created that character." That attitude was especially irritating to writers because the only true creators are the writers. To create by definition means to "bring into being from nothing." The writer was the only person in television, movies, or the theatre who started from nothing. The pages were blank until the writer got an idea and typed it onto the page.

From that point on, everyone was adapting. The actor molded the character that the writer created. The director added form to the scenario and the dialogue that the writer created. Everyone after the writer had a script to go on.

So it was annoying when performers claimed ownership of a character.

In their defense, they were talented people who breathed life into words that writers gave them, but they didn't create characters; they interpreted them.

For all those reasons, we were glad to get away from writing situation comedies.

We wanted to pattern Tim's show after the popular Marty Feldman variety show and the Benny Hill shows. We wanted to have a lot of activity on the screen to keep the hour moving and exciting. So we did a lot of short bits and runners and shot most of them on location. It was fun, but it was also troublesome.

We shot a series of golfing gags at Griffith Park. Bill and I wanted to be on camera, and as producers, we could hire ourselves to be on camera, so we did. We were in the first line of spectators watching the action on the green as Tim Conway was putting. However, it began to drizzle, and then it began to pour. We got soaked. However, we continued shooting anytime there was even a slight break in the deluge.

Soon, Bill and I wanted to get ourselves off camera. It was much more pleasant to send other people out to be extras in the scene while we remained comfortably in our trailer. You would think as producers who could put themselves on camera, we would have taken ourselves off camera, but we couldn't because we were in the first shot and the following ones had to match. So each time the rain let up, we had to march out and be in the same spot for each shot.

Sometimes we paid a price to satisfy our egos.

We shot at the beach. We shot at a vacant bank and department store in South Pasadena. We shot in the center of Los Angeles where many of the silent movie comedies were filmed.

We even shot in the CBS parking lot. The premise of that bit was that Tim was backing his car out and was doing such a bad job of it that he had traffic totally stalled in the lot. People started to honk their horns. Tim then began to conduct all the horn blowers. He led them as a conductor would lead an orchestra, and indeed, the random horn blowing became a symphony.

The soundman on the show did a masterful job. He recorded

many different car horns, then categorized them as to what musical note they were, then he arranged them so that they played a tune. It was very skillful and turned out to be a unique, funny sketch.

Of course, we also did the sketches, runners, and bits in the studio, too. Some of the people in the cast were from radio. They had a very successful advertising business and were a big success in radio. They wrote their own radio commercials, so they wanted to write some sketches, too.

One of them came in one day with a sketch idea. She read it to us, and every so often she said, "Put something funny in here." After a while, we stopped her and said, "You know, the 'put something funny in here' is the real writing. If you want to do a sketch for the show, you put the 'something funny' in and then show it to us."

Our primary goal was to get Tim Conway renewed. He had starred in several variety shows and sitcoms, but none had been picked up for the second year. He was on *McHale's Navy* for many seasons, but it wasn't his show. The gag around town was that they should have Tim Conway star in the Vietnam War. That way, it would be over in 13 weeks. It was such a running gag that Tim had a personalized license plate that read, "13 WKS."

We got off to a good start. We had a good writing staff, Tim had a lot of input, and the short gags and runners worked nicely. We were very proud of our inaugural show. After the taping, we ran into a CBS executive, who said to Bill Richmond and me, "You know what's wrong with this show? Some parts of it are funnier than others."

We said, "That's a shame. We tried to keep them all the same amount of funny."

It was a dumb, but typical statement. We couldn't always have the same level of intensity in humor—in fact, in anything. Even if we could accomplish that, it would have been self-defeating because it would have made the humor monotonous. The glory of humor was that the laughter erupted in certain spots. The artistry of it was in designing those ideas that lead up to the big laughs. That executive missed the point entirely.

One drawback on the show was that the production staff and the crew were all professionals from *The Carol Burnett Show,* but the cast wasn't. The magic that happened or evolved on her show wasn't happening on his. The performers were good, but as a unit, they didn't have what Carol's cast had. That caused us some problems as producers.

Before one musical number, we spoke to the female performer and told her to relax and do that bit as herself. It was a song that was reminiscent of Carol Burnett, but we didn't want her to do a caricature of Carol. We encouraged her to bring her own style to the song.

She rushed into her trailer in tears, feeling that we had accused her of not being as good as Carol, but we had done no such thing. We could have; she wasn't Carol. We simply didn't want her to try to be Carol.

Another cast member sometimes disrupted the sketches by adlibbing in the middle of them. He'd "break the fourth wall." If something unexpected happened, that performer stepped out of character and either joked to other cast members or to the audience.

Bill and I had a talk with him and asked him to refrain from doing that. He got very upset at us, saying, "Harvey Korman did that all the time on *The Carol Burnett Show* and nobody ever got upset with him." He had a point, but then the reality hit us—Harvey always adlibbed in character. That's what made the difference. If Harvey was playing a gangster and a picture unexpectedly fell off the wall, Harvey would do a joke, but as a gangster. If he was playing a werewolf and somebody missed a cue, Harvey would chastise him or her as a werewolf. He never came out of character. I'm not sure, though, that the other actor ever really accepted our explanation.

Tim's show was never quite the same as the old Carol Burnett show, but it was good television entertainment, and we did get Tim Conway partly renewed. CBS picked the show up for the next season, but as a half-hour show instead of a full-hour show.

The network thinking was that *The Carol Burnett Show* was trimmed down to a half-hour and sold into syndication and it was doing well. They thought a half-hour of Tim Conway comedy would be tighter and funnier than the hour show.

Again, executive thinking, like the guy who thought all comedy should be the same amount of funny. Those executives thought that since Carol's show condensed nicely to a half-hour, then Tim's would be more effective in the half-hour format. The difference was that Carol's was trimmed down after it was in the can. It was Monday morning quarterbacking. Once the show was shot, we knew where the funniest pieces were. We could trim down to them and make the show more compact and even funnier than the original. We couldn't pick out the best of a show that hadn't been taped yet. Comedy was guesswork and we were only guessing at which the funniest half-hour was.

Nevertheless, the network cut the show back to a half-hour. Then, the problem was that they wanted all of us working on the show to reduce our salaries proportionally. They wanted us to work at half of what we had signed on for. Again, the executive logic was that if a show was only half of what it was before, we only had to work half as hard. Not so. In fact, we probably had to work harder to deliver a fair amount of laughs in a smaller amount of time.

Someone asked Mark Twain to give a talk once and asked how long it would take him to prepare. He asked, "How long do I have to speak?" They asked why that mattered. Twain said (and I'm paraphrasing), "If you want me to talk for an hour, I can have it ready in an hour. If you want me to speak for ten minutes, I'll need a week to prepare."

Bill and I refused the salary cut. We had a contract. If the network wanted the show, they'd have to honor that contract. The contract also called for us to get an increase for the second season.

Joe Hamilton was somewhat shocked. He said he didn't care about the money because it was not his money, but the network's. It wouldn't cost him or save him anything regardless of what we agreed to with the network. However, he did say, "Look, if you do this for them, they'll owe you a favor."

I objected to that. Again, it was that same erroneous executive logic. I asked Joe, "When do we collect the favor?"

He didn't know what I meant.

I said, "If we do a great job this second season and make this show a hit, they'll want us no matter what. Hiring us then, is not a favor, but if we screw it up and destroy the show, they won't give us another chance. They'd replace us in an instant." I didn't say it, but I thought, *they'd probably use the money they're saving on our salaries to get new producers.* So again I asked, "When do we collect on the favor?"

Joe had no answer for that because there was no answer. Getting an IOU from a network was like having Jack the Ripper walk us home at night.

We held our ground. The only compromise we made was that we agreed to forego our increase. However, losing a 10 percent increase was preferable to losing 50 percent of our salary.

Towards the end of the second season of the Conway show, I had symptoms and a stress test that showed cardio-vascular problems. I had open-heart surgery before the season ended.

The production crew sent a large frog made of green candy to the hospital after the surgery. The card read, "Don't croak."

Effectively, I was off the show for the last several weeks of production and it looked like that would be the last year of the show. Cancellation seemed to be a definite possibility. I was not supposed to go back to work, but I did get an okay to be there for the last rehearsal of the season and the writers meeting that followed.

I was the running straight gag for the meeting. Tim said, "I don't know, this sketch seems to be dying—whoops—sorry, Gene." "I don't want to make too many changes because it would cut the heart out of the sketch—whoops—no offense, Gene."

I outlived the show. It was dropped at the end of that second season.

Chapter Nineteen
Mama's Family

Most of the writers on *The Carol Burnett Show* hated the "Eunice" sketches except for Dick Clair and Jenna McMahon who created them. Actually, they wrote one sketch for Roddy McDowell, which Carol loved playing and that evolved into the series of "Eunice" sketches.

In that first sketch, McDowell played a very successful author, who was Eunice's brother and Mama Harper's son. He wrote for major magazines and had just come from an interview with Queen Elizabeth II. However, none of the family was impressed. They were more interested and fascinated with the new trick that the family dog had just learned.

The sketch played well and Carol loved the Eunice character. She was a self-centered, shrill, jealous woman, who hated her brothers, her sisters, and her Mama.

The writers hated the sketches because the characters were so unlikable, and also because the sketches started so high. The characters were yelling at each other from the very start for trifling reasons, consequently, they had no room to build.

However, few of the writers were involved in the sketches because Dick and Jenna wrote all of them. They felt a certain amount of ownership over those characters. It got to the point where those sketches were all that Dick and Jenna wrote, and they wrote long, rambling sketches. Ed Simmons hated those pieces for the above reasons, but also because he was the one who had to harness the characters and control Dick and Jenna and their tendency to overwrite.

Nevertheless, the sketches were popular and became a regular part of the show. A few years after the show went off the air, Joe Hamilton, in conjunction with Dick and Jenna, sold the concept to CBS as a pilot called *Mama's Family*.

Dick and Jenna were to write and produce the series. The problem was that when Dick and Jenna were in charge, they had no one to harness their efforts. They wanted to write until the show was perfect. They wrote and wrote and delivered nothing to the network. The show was scheduled to air at a certain date, and Dick and Jenna were delivering no scripts and hiring no actors for the part. They weren't producing a show.

CBS got after them, but Dick and Jenna went into isolation. They didn't return calls and couldn't be reached. In desperation, Joe Hamilton hired Ed Simmons to get the writing and the show organized and ready for production on schedule. Ed brought in Rick Hawkins and Liz Sage, who had worked with him on the Burnett show, and the production began to take shape. At least, a cast was hired and scripts were readied for rehearsal and shooting. Dick and Jenna just disappeared, except to collect royalties for creating the show.

On reflection, the other Burnett writers should have objected to that arrangement. We should have shared in the revenue. Admittedly, Dick and Jenna wrote all of the "Eunice" sketches, but the other writers took up the slack by writing enough sketches for the Burnett show to allow Dick and Jenna to write only the "Eunice" sketches. Also, I believed that when characters were created for a show, all of the writers should have shared in the ownership of those characters regardless of which specific writers first wrote the character. However, none of us pursued it, and Dick and Jenna reaped the rewards.

The show was successful. It was a softer version of the "Eunice" sketches. It was more of a sitcom, whereas the sketches on the Burnett show were very broad and much more suited to a variety show than a weekly situation comedy.

I wasn't involved with the beginning of the show. I came on after the show had been established for a few weeks.

I was still recovering from heart surgery when the Conway show was cancelled, so I wasn't very aggressive in finding other work. Most of the shows had already been staffed by the time I was ready to go back into action. That made finding work more difficult. It was the first time since I began in television in 1969 that the jobs became hard to find.

Bill and I did get work on a pilot, though. It was an Angie Dickinson show that was created and being produced by Alan Katz for Johnny Carson's production company. We signed on as producers.

Alan Katz had written the pilot episode. We worked on the rewrite of that, but also began lining up writers to do other episodes. We wrote a couple of those episodes, too.

However, the pilot show didn't go well. Angie wasn't happy with it. She shot it, but she wasn't at all pleased with it. When it came time to produce the second show in the series, Angie had gone to Tahiti or some such remote place.

We had a meeting with Johnny Carson and a viewing of the first show with him. He didn't have many suggestions except to recognize that Angie Dickinson was unhappy with her character and the direction the show was taking.

We listened and offered suggestions of our own, but nothing mattered. Angie was not going to do the show. Production was stopped and we were out of a job. However, we still had a contract. We would be paid for thirteen shows whether they were produced or not. That's what we thought.

Carson's production company came up with another show called *Teacher's Lounge.* They asked us to meet with Aaron Ruben, the executive producer. Bill, I, Rick Hawkins, and Liz Sage met with Aaron one morning and he explained the concept of the show to us. The meeting lasted all morning, and when we broke for lunch, Aaron felt that we would return with a positive response. Bill and I would produce the show and Rick and Liz would be on the writing staff.

However, the more the four of us discussed it over lunch, the more it seemed like an unworkable idea. It took place in a lounge and all of the action would be talked about rather than seen. We returned and told Aaron that we weren't interested in doing it. He was stunned, disappointed, and angry.

Then, our checks stopped coming.

Johnny Carson's business people claimed that by turning down that show, we had violated our Angie Dickinson contract, so they weren't required to pay off our deal. We, of course, rejected that premise and took our complaint to the Writers Guild.

The Carson people agreed to meet with Bill and me to try to settle the dispute. They claimed it was the same show as the Angie Dickinson show and that we reneged. We claimed it was an entirely different concept with an entirely different cast and a different executive producer, and that it bore no resemblance to the show that we had agreed to produce. They were forced to agree with that and were to pay us our contracted salary for the thirteen weeks.

However, they would not pay us for the scripts we wrote that were not produced. We said that we agreed to write those in good faith, we delivered the pages, and we should be paid. Apparently, they had a major disagreement with Alan Katz. They claimed that they didn't contract for the shows; he did. We argued that if they had a dispute with Alan Katz, it should be litigated with Alan Katz. He hired us to write those shows and he was a representative of their company when he hired us. We delivered. We should be paid. Again, they reluctantly agreed and paid us for our work. That was the end of the Angie Dickinson pilot.

It was settled to our satisfaction, but left us looking for work again at a time when it was hard to find work. All the jobs were filled.

I called Bill Richmond with a couple of ideas to pursue. He said, "Maybe it's better if we go our separate ways." That was okay with me and I quickly agreed. We ended our writing partnership.

I called Ed Simmons to see if there were any openings on *Mama's Family*. Ed immediately found space for me on the staff, but caused me to do something that I've regretted ever since.

Then, the negotiations proved my point about "returning favors," such as the discussion that we had with Joe Hamilton when the Conway show was reduced to a half-hour format. Joe Hamilton was to hire me, but at almost the minimum wage. I had been one of the major writers on the Burnett show for five seasons when the staff collected three Emmy Awards. I had been the producer of the Tim Conway show for two years. Then, when I needed work, I was held over a barrel and signed for a much reduced salary.

So much for the "they'll owe you a favor" concept.

The sitcom featured Vicki Lawrence as "Mama," the role she originated on *The Carol Burnett Show*. Ken Berry played her son, "Vinnie." Eunice and Ed had moved on to Florida to begin a new life, but their children stayed home and lived with their grandmother, Mama Harper.

Vicki was a delight to work with. She was the star of this show and she carried it well. She was not overly demanding. She contributed many ideas to the show, was willing to listen to the staff's suggestions, and she appreciated the writing.

I was not thrilled to be back in situation comedy for all the reasons that I outlined before. Nevertheless, that was a good show. I liked the characters. Mama especially had appeal because she seemed to represent someone to everyone. She was every viewer's grandma, aunt, sister, or someone. She had a universal appeal. I enjoyed writing those shows.

The executive logic, though, tainted that show, too. At one time, we were trying to outline and write several shows in advance. Ed Simmons had some ideas that he offered to the writers. I liked one of them and offered to write it. Ed said, "Fine."

One thing that I liked to do with stories was to let them simmer. I just thought about them for awhile and tossed ideas around in my head, not accepting or rejecting any of them, but let them just occupy my mind. Then, one or two of the ideas jelled and I started formulating the plot and some of the jokes to go along with it.

However, once I agreed to write that story, Ed Simmons handed me a plot outline. I said, "What's this?"

Ed said, "That's the plot outline for the story you're going to write."

I said, "No, I like to develop the plot on my own."

Ed said, "Well, this is the one I submitted to the network and they approved it."

I said, "Then you write it."

I refused to write that particular episode because the fun of the writing was taken from me.

Mama, the character, was a lovable soul, but she had her faults. She was overbearing, almost dictatorial. She raised Eunice, which also raised doubt about her parenting credentials.

I wondered whether she was a good mother or not.

Because of those doubts about her parenting skills, I came up with a story concept in which there was a catastrophe of some sort in Raytown, the mythical town where they lived. It would probably be a flood, a huge fire, or some such disaster that would cause many people to be homeless. I wanted Mama to offer her house to a poor family that was rendered homeless as a result of the tragedy.

The idea of the story was that Mama and the mother of the other family would butt heads over who was the better parent. It would show that a low income household could have love and discipline as much as the Harper family could. In fact, it might even show that the indigent woman might give some lessons to Mama on how to be a worthwhile mother.

Before I wrote it, the network got involved. They felt the concept was so strong that it should feature a major star such as Sally Fields or Meryl Streep. "Write it for someone like that," they said.

I objected. If we got Sally Fields or Meryl Streep or anyone with that sort of stature, the script would have to be written for them. It would become a major role.

"That's what we want," the network insisted.

"But you'll never get Sally Fields or Meryl Streep or anyone coming close to those credentials," I said. "Then you'll be stuck with a story demanding a major star and no major star to fill the role."

"Just write it and let us worry about getting the star," the network ordered.

So I wrote the story with a strong part for Sally, Meryl, or whomever.

Of course, Sally Fields and Meryl Streep were not available to do a television situation comedy. The network asked us to come up with alternatives. We suggested Cher, Angie Dickinson, and a host of other people. The network couldn't coax any of them into doing it, either.

Then, the command degenerated to "Get somebody like Sally Fields or Meryl Streep." Whatever names we offered, though, the network rejected because they were *like* Fields or Streep, but they *weren't* Fields or Streep.

Next, the idea was to find relative newcomers with the potential to become a Sally Fields or a Meryl Streep. That was an impossible task because networks didn't recognize potential; they saw only marquee value. Consequently, any name we suggested was dismissed.

The end result was what I had predicted when the original "Get Fields or Streep" edict was issued—the show was dropped because the part of the second mother was written for a major star and we could not deliver a major star.

Executive logic, again.

The executives almost shot down another episode. I had an idea for a show that centered on a concept that hit close to my personal life. My mother's generation believed in visiting gravesites regularly, but I didn't. So, I worked that into a *Mama's Family* episode.

The network wasn't keen on the idea. It probably featured ideas that they didn't subscribe to, and it also dealt with a depressing topic—death. However, we got an okay to go ahead with the script. The script was strong.

We originally shot the cemetery scene in the studio, but when the network saw the final version of the show, they insisted that we reshoot the cemetery scene outdoors. They wanted it to look authentic. Frankly the indoor scene was very phony because you could see the seams of the fake grass.

The basic idea was that Mama visited her long departed husband, Carl, at his gravesite each week and she talked openly with him as if he was there beside her. Then, she noticed that the grave next to his, the one reserved for her, had a headstone with another woman's name on it.

Mama got furious and started pounding Carl's tombstone with her purse and accusing him of having an "affair" with that woman.

It was certainly my favorite script for that show and may be the best situation comedy script I ever wrote.

Another favorite of mine was a script I did parodying the popular show of the time, *The People's Court* with Judge Wopner. In that episode, Mama borrowed a vacuum cleaner that was given to Vint and Naomi as a wedding gift. When she used it, it snagged on her heirloom rug and burned a giant hole in it. Mama sued Naomi for negligence, and Naomi countersued because Mama borrowed her property without permission and destroyed it.

We tried to get Judge Wopner to play himself, but he refused.

However, the play worked just as well with an actor in the role. It was a very funny script.

However, after the Wednesday run-through, Vicki came to the

writers meeting and wanted the script redone. For whatever reason, she objected to the script centering on a vacuum cleaner. "Why couldn't it be a hairdryer?" she asked. I have no idea why Vicki felt so strongly opposed to the idea of the vacuum cleaner, but she was.

However, that was on a Wednesday and we were to shoot the show on Friday. Nevertheless, Vicki wanted a rewrite with the vacuum cleaner removed. Joe Hamilton did his homework and pointed out that it wasn't a simple task to just change the appliance. Vicki wanted to know why. Joe pointed out that just changing that one item would require about 146 changes in the script. No way could a new script be completed in time for the shooting.

Vicki pouted, but Joe pulled rank. The story went as scripted and it was a very funny segment.

However, that argument was the final straw for me. I had had it with situation comedy and stars of situation comedies. I resigned using the excuse that I had a speaking career starting up and I wanted to be free to travel at any time. They gave me my release.

In effect, I was done with television writing except for the Bob Hope specials. I signed on as a full-time writer with Bob Hope to the exclusion of any other television writing.

Chapter Twenty
Summer Replacements

The television season used to be fairly regular. We did twenty-six shows over thirty-six weeks. That gave us a few non-production weeks throughout the season to either catch up on scripts that had fallen behind, or to take a few weeks off to recover from overwork. Of course, it also left us sixteen weeks of hiatus.

Writers used the hiatus in various ways. Some simply vacationed. Others took it as an opportunity to write that screenplay they had always wanted to write or to create a show of their own. Sometimes, writers used that time to find more work on summer replacement shows.

I worked on a couple of summer shows. The first was the *Helen Reddy Show* in the summer of 1973. It was a replacement for Flip Wilson's variety show and was produced by Flip's company.

Flip showed up occasionally to talk with the writers and make some semblance of being an executive producer. Mostly we just sat around and had a few laughs. After the show ended, though, Flip Wilson got in some sort of trouble for brandishing a gun and chasing his in-laws out of the house.

I wasn't too crazy about writing material for a guy who was armed.

Helen was a very hot vocalist at that time and she attracted some good guests. One was Jim Croce. His rehearsal was one of the most memorable of any show I've ever been associated with. He and his band set up to do their number and they played "Bad, Bad Leroy Brown." Croce sang such a lively rendition that everyone in the rehearsal hall was clapping along and tapping their toes. It was probably the most astounding performance I've ever seen at any rehearsal or any show I've ever attended.

A few months later, Jim Croce was killed in the tragic plane accident.

Helen Reddy's big hit, "I Am Woman," was sort of the national anthem for the feminist movement. The producer of that show was Carolyn Raskin. One of the guests we had was Gloria Steinem.

I worked with Ray Taylor as my partner on that show. He and I got to Burbank Studios early one morning because we were scheduled to have a meeting and script reading with Gloria, who was flying in from New York.

She didn't arrive at the scheduled time. She didn't arrive two hours after the scheduled time. She arrived about five or six hours late for the rehearsal. Nevertheless, we were all cordial when she arrived, with the possible exception of Ray Taylor. He was aloof.

As we read through the script, Gloria removed the gender from any word she could. "Hostess" was changed to "host." "Chairman" was changed to "chairperson." Ray and I joked among ourselves that if we had written the word "manhole cover" into the script, she would have altered it to "personhole cover." She neutered everything.

Towards the end of the meeting, Gloria objected to a certain joke line, not because it was anti-feminine, but because it wasn't funny enough. Ray Taylor bristled.

Carolyn Raskin turned to him and whispered, "Let's get a new joke there."

Ray said, "What's wrong with the joke that's already there?"

Carolyn said, "We might make it funnier."

Ray said, "That's a funny joke as it is."

Carolyn said, "Well, let's try some alternatives."

Ray said, "We don't need any alternatives. That's a good joke."

Finally Carolyn leaned toward Ray and whispered secretively about Gloria, "She doesn't like it."

Ray said loudly and not so secretively, "You mean *it* doesn't like it."

With that, he got up, left the meeting, and never returned to the show. It didn't make any difference. The show never had much impact.

In 1976, Bob Tamplin, an executive at CBS, asked Ed Simmons, Bill Richmond, and I to go see Kelly Monteith, a young comedian at the Horn, a club in Santa Monica. Bob was trying to get him a summer show on the network schedule.

We saw him and liked him. We were willing to create a summer variety show for him. We did the show with most of the Carol Burnett team: Ed Simmons produced and Bill Richmond and I wrote along with Rick Hawkins and Liz Sage.

Again, the show didn't amount to much. Kelly was funny and likeable, but the show didn't impress either the executives or the viewing audience.

Probably the highlight of the short four-week season was getting the opportunity to work with George Gobel. I always admired Gobel when his show was hot. I found him to be a naturally funny man and a delight to work with.

We also had Freddy Prinze as a guest. He was okay to work with. He wasn't as personable as Gobel, but he wasn't a thorn in the side, either. It was not long after that Freddy shot himself.

Again, I would have hesitated had I known I was working with a guy who carried a gun.

I didn't do any summer replacement shows after that. They were too heavily armed.

Chapter Twenty-One
The Bob Hope Experience

While I worked on all of the shows I've already written about, I was also writing material for Bob Hope's television specials and personal appearances. The Hope work provided extra income during those years, but that wasn't the primary reason why I was happy to accept the assignment. I wrote for Bob Hope, and for a while, I also wrote for Phyllis Diller, both so that I could keep my writing sharp and funny.

Television writing was usually a compromise, and the individual writer rarely had any pride of authorship. It's writing by committee. Even if I wrote something on my own, it was under the supervision of the producers of the show. There was usually input from the other writers, the director, the stars, and maybe the executives, and their ideas were all combined by the time it became a script and appeared on a screen.

Even if no one else added a word of dialogue to my script, they invariably add input, direction, and notes of some sort or another. The writing might have been mine, but it was guided by the direction of others. I felt all of that weakened my material. To illustrate, on the Nabors show, we were doing a routine about the phoniness of Hollywood and how you could never trust anything in Tinseltown to be real. At one of the writers meetings, I ad-libbed a gag: "You can't believe anything you see in the movies. I don't know whether you know it or not, but John Wayne sleeps with a night light."

It got a big laugh in the room and the producers immediately penciled it into the script.

After a minute or two, one of the writers objected. "You know, sleeping with a night light doesn't necessarily mean that a person is a sissy." That didn't matter because the perception was that it did. People listening to the gag immediately understood the concept and laughed at it. Nevertheless, the writers then began to accommodate that writer's objection. "How about, 'John Wayne is so afraid of the dark that he sleeps with a night light?'" "John Wayne always asks to sleep with his Mommy."

They began to explain the joke so much that the humor was lost. Finally, the producers took it out of the script after overanalyzing the logic of the joke, all because one writer, who probably did sleep with a night light, felt that the joke offended his manhood and rebelled.

Many times, the producers said about some of my lines, "That's a *think* joke." That irritated me somewhat because, to me, all good jokes are think jokes. The audience thought about it, understood it, and that produced the laugh. As far as I was concerned, taking the *think* out of a joke also took the *joke* out of a joke.

I also learned very quickly that TV writers never wrote any weak material. At least in their opinion, they didn't. There were always other excuses why material didn't work. The lighting was wrong. The set was not right for the material. The actor read it wrong. The director shot it wrong. The audience wasn't paying attention. Rarely was it the fault of the writer.

With one-liner writing for comedians like Bob Hope and Phyllis Diller, the joke was presented to the audience. If it got screams, it was a great line. If it didn't, it wasn't. It was that simple and that honest.

For me, television writing was unsatisfying.

Phyllis offered me a preview of what was to come when I told her I had been hired to work in network television. She said, "Don't become a fat-ass Hollywood writer." During my first season on a staff, I began to see what she meant. In fact, I had a desk piece made with the engraving "DBAFAHW" on it. It was a constant reminder to me to keep the writing sharp and not become a fat-ass Hollywood writer.

That's why I wrote for Hope.

Here's how I wrote for him: Bob called and requested material on some subject. Usually, it was something in the news, or something that was being talked about by everyone. Sometimes, though, it was a more esoteric subject. For example, he once called and wanted material about some man whose name I didn't recognize. Bob said, "Oh, he used to play cards with General Eisenhower during the war."

One time, Bob called and wanted material about psychiatrists. He was doing a convention for them and wanted some jokes aimed specifically at them. Well, writing for psychiatrists was easy. However, when I tried to call the gags in to Bob, he said, "Oh, I made a mistake. It's not a psychiatrists' convention. It's chiropractors." That meant writing a whole new batch of jokes in a hurry.

I made it a personal discipline to always write at least thirty gags on any topic that Bob gave me, unless of course, I didn't have the time. Often, Bob called, gave me some information, and said, "Write me some jokes. I'll call you back in about ten minutes." Well, in that case, I wrote what I could in ten minutes. Bob always called on time.

When the phone rang and I picked it up, he wouldn't say "Hello" or "How are you?" He'd simply say, "Thrill me."

He just wanted the jokes.

I set a personal goal of at least thirty jokes for a several reasons. I wanted to show Bob that I could produce, that I could turn out a good quantity of quality jokes in a hurry. Some of the other writers objected. "You're writing so much that it makes it tough on us." Again, I remembered Phyllis Diller's admonition, "Don't become a fat ass Hollywood writer," and I kept turning out a good amount of material. If they were worried about their jobs, I believed that they should then write more.

Second, I felt that by writing more jokes, I wrote better jokes. If Bob had thirty of my gags to chose from, he'd select more of my gags.

In order to write that many, I divided the topic up into sub-topics. If the material was about the President's State of the Union Address, I listed the main topics he talked about, what the opposing party thought of it, how the television stations covered it, how it might affect us as citizens, how it might affect other nations, and so on. Then, I wrote five or six gags on each of the sub-topics, and eventually, I had a routine of thirty to thirty-five jokes on the main topic.

I wrote the jokes in any order. For instance, my first joke might have been about taxes, which might have been the first sub-topic. The next joke might have been about France's reaction to the speech, which might have been my fifth sub-topic. I just kept writing gags in random order.

When I'd typed enough jokes, I cut them into individual pieces and arranged them into separate piles according to sub-topics. Then, I arranged each of the jokes in a sub-topic in a logical order, and rewrote any that needed rewriting in order to keep a natural, conversational flow going. Then, I put the sub-topics into a logical order, again rewriting wherever it was needed to maintain the conversational rhythm. Finally, I retyped the jokes and submitted them to Bob. When computers came into existence, they made that "cut and paste" process quicker and easier, but in the beginning, I literally cut, pasted, and retyped.

The process was time consuming, but it made the writing of the gags easier and it made the final product much more organized. It worked, too, because Bob commented once that he could use my material as it was written. He said, "Whatever you're doing, keep on doing it." So I did.

To further emphasize my frustration with television writing, I once used that same process to write a piece for Frank Sutton on the Nabors show. When one producer came in and saw the small pieces of paper scattered all over my desk while I was rearranging them into neat, logical piles, he went through the roof. "Why are you wasting all this time?"

I said, "It makes the routine more logical."

"Just put numbers beside each joke," he said.

That would work, too, for some. For me, it was too distracting to keep searching back and forth through the collection of gags to see which number came next and so on. By arranging them in order, I was free to shuffle them around, rearrange them easily, and see the results more clearly and more quickly.

However, the producer insisted I not waste time by doing this, so I didn't. I didn't want to waste valuable writing time while the higher paid writers in the next room were busy playing darts.

Bob Hope's method of using writers had another fringe benefit for me. He always wanted the material quickly. "Here's the topic, now where are the jokes?" He wasn't demanding, dictatorial, or unpleasant about it. It was just that he wanted results. His writers had to be able to produce funny material on demand.

Consequently, there was no time to allow myself the luxury of writer's block. I had to turn out material, so I did. It was that simple.

Phil Lasker, whowas another of Bob Hope's writers for a short time, said, "You can turn in good material to Bob Hope or you can turn in bad material to Bob Hope, but you can't turn in *no* material to Bob Hope." I had to put something on the pages, so I wrote. I didn't have time to put it off, feel sorry for myself, or to wander about my office moaning, "There's nothing funny about this topic." I just wrote.

Phil Lasker also had a funny take on writer's block. He claimed that writers were the only people who could enjoy this luxury. He said, "Suppose you're on your way to a meeting in San Francisco. You get off the plane, grab your luggage, and hop into a cab. You tell the driver, 'Take me to the St. Francis hotel.' The driver says, 'Oh, I'm sorry. I've got cab driver's block. I can't take you there.' You'd hit him over the head with your briefcase." Phil's point was that there's no such thing as "Cab Driver's Block," and there was truly no such thing as writer's block among Bob's writers.

When Bob was traveling, he'd often call from wherever he was with some interesting local angle or a new topic that he wanted to do that night. I'd work on it, and then read the jokes to him over the phone. Normally, he'd listen and evaluate the gags as I read. "Check that one," he'd say.

When I was done reading the gags, I read the checked ones back to him. He either copied them down or memorized them and used them that evening. Once, I was on the phone with him and he wasn't making any comments about the material. I said, "Do you want me to check any of these?"

He said, "Just keep reading . . . keep reading."

So, I continued to read the gags. Then, over the phone, I heard the orchestra playing "Thanks for the Memory." An announcer said, "Ladies and gentlemen, Bob Hope."

Bob said into the phone, "I've got to go now. I'm on."

He hung up, went onstage, and presumably did some of the lines I had just read to him.

Bob loved material, lots of it. Whenever he traveled, there were two things he wanted constantly by his side—his makeup case and his briefcase full of pages of jokes. He refused to drive off in his limousine unless both of those items were safely in the car with him.

He loved quantity. I believe that's why I did so well with Bob. I wrote fast, I wrote a lot, and I wrote well, too.

When I handed an envelope full of material to Bob, he wouldn't open it immediately. He hefted it in his hands to check its weight. If it was heavy enough, he'd say, "That's good." He was kidding, of course, but the writer did get the idea that he wanted a goodly amount of jokes.

Bob was understanding, too. Once, I handed him a batch of material and he asked me, "Is this brilliant?"

I gave him an honest answer. I said, "To tell you the truth, Bob, it's not."

He said, "Oh well, some of the other guys will be on."

Bob appreciated writers and the work they did for him and his career. At an interview for his ninetieth birthday telecast, someone asked him, "You've had many great writers over the years. Could you have accomplished what you have without those writers?"

Bob answered with a quip. "I never needed writers . . . unless, of course, I wanted to say something."

Then, he gave a serious reply. He said, "I know show business and I know comedy. I would have made it without writers, but I never would have made it big time."

Once, Bob and I sat in his dressing room discussing a particular joke. He wanted it to read one way and I argued that it should go a different way. We discussed it for some time, and I finally said, "Why are we going back and forth like this? We both know you're going to win the argument."

Bob pointed a finger at me and said, "Don't ever think like that. I hire you because you know what you're talking about and I want you to give me your opinion straight out."

Nevertheless, I think he did win the argument.

That was a nice thing to say to a writer, but it wasn't the biggest compliment I ever got from Bob. One time, he asked me to write a song for one of his specials. Reluctantly, I did. I felt he should get professional song writers to do that, but he insisted that I give it a try.

I wrote the lyrics, picked out the melody on my guitar, sang it into a tape recorder, and presented it to Bob. Before he played the tape, he asked, "Is this brilliant?"

I said, "Bob, if I could write great song lyrics, would I be spending my time writing comedy?"

He gave me a serious look and said, "I think you would, Gene. I really think you would."

I've always cherished that remark.

The song that he forced me to write played great on the show. It was nominated for an Emmy for "Original Music." It didn't win, but it was nice to get the nomination.

Working with Bob was like getting a PhD in comedy, not only on stage, but also in handling audiences and people offstage, too. One thing I learned in working with him was not to be too demanding of myself.

When he was doing a special from the Montreal Olympics, he asked me to write a parody of "Put It There, Pal" for him and Bing Crosby. I was thrilled. Those were two of my show business idols. I had met Crosby when I worked on the Burnett show, but I had never written for him. That opportunity delighted me.

However, the material I turned out didn't delight me. I was disappointed in my efforts and I told Bob that when I handed the piece to him.

I didn't travel to Montreal with the show because I was working on the staff of other shows. However, I watched the telecast. The musical parody of "Put It There, Pal" was sung by Bob and Bing exactly as I had written it, and it was the highlight of the show.

I was stunned, and I realized two things: first, Hope and Crosby added luster to material that wasn't sparkling on paper. Second, we professional joke writers, even when we are off, are still pretty damned good.

That gave me a renewed confidence in my writing.

Bob worked the writers hard, but he had no qualms about that because he felt he paid us well, and he did.

One year, we finished taping the last special of the season. All of us writers gathered in Bob's dressing room to say our goodbyes. As Bob was changing, he said to us, "I'm going to Notre Dame next week. Get me some football jokes, will you?"

One of the writers said, "Bob, we've been doing football jokes all season. You haven't used a lot of them. Use some of them at Notre Dame. You don't need new jokes."

Hope thought about that for a second, went right up to that particular writer and said, "I pay you with new money, don't I?"

We all wrote new football jokes.

Bob called any time of the day or night on any day of the week, including weekends and holidays. We wrote when he called. Once, he told me that he was going on a fishing trip to Alaska. He said he'd be in a remote spot without telephones and he'd be gone for two to three weeks.

I and all the other writers were delighted. For us, it was a two or three-week vacation.

Then about three days later, Bob called me and asked for some material. I said, "I thought you were off fishing in Alaska."

He said, "I came home. I found out fish don't applaud."

Bob also taught me the value of a sense of humor.

The first time I went over to Bob's house in Toluca Lake, I walked into the game room. It was a small room with a billiard table in the center. However, there was no pool playing that day because the entire pool table was covered with a model of the home that the Hope's were planning to build in Palm Springs.

Bob lifted the roof off the model and showed me what each of the rooms would be and where the indoor swimming pool was to be. It was fascinating.

Later, they began to build that house in the desert.

I was on the phone with Bob one day when he said, "Hold on. I've got a call on the other line."

I held on, but Bob never did return to the call. I eventually hung up, but later I saw why he didn't return. On the news, they reported that the house under construction in Palm Springs had caught fire and was almost totally destroyed.

The next day, he called back and apologized for leaving me hanging on the phone. "Did you hear what happened?" he asked.

I told him I had and how sorry I was about it.

He said, "Do some jokes about it."

I said, "What? How can you do jokes about something like that?"

He said, "Well, it's good that it happened before we moved in. That could have been a real tragedy. Besides, people are going to be expecting me to say something about it. I need some jokes."

So, I wrote some gags about his house being destroyed. Later that day, he quoted one of the jokes on a news broadcast: "It's a terrible feeling to wake up in the morning and find out that the black cloud hanging over your home in Los Angeles used to be your home in Palm Springs."

Bob taught me a bit about the psychology of humor, too. We were taping a monologue for one of his specials and we had written some material about President Gerald Ford and his football playing days.

Bob always did his monologues right before the show aired so that the material was as current as possible. He borrowed Johnny Carson's audience for those. After Carson's show was completed, Bob asked the audience to stay if they wanted to see his monologue. Everyone stayed.

For the live audience, Bob did about 150 gags on various topics. Then, we edited those down to about fifty jokes for the monologue that would air on the show.

One particular evening, he did a lot of his material and then announced to the audience that he was going to take a short break. He told them, "We're going to do a short piece that's going to air at the White House. It's a few jokes about Gerry Ford and his football playing days. Hang around. I think you'll enjoy it."

When Bob came offstage, I asked, "When did this White House gig come up? I didn't know anything about it."

Bob said, "There's no White House show. The audience was getting tired, so I wanted them to take a little break. Besides, if they think they're part of something that's being shown at the White House, they'll be more enthused about it."

He went back and did the football material to a full audience and it played beautifully.

I enjoyed a long and exciting career—almost thirty years—working with Bob on his concerts, military trips, and NBC specials. Working with him was often demanding and challenging, but it was always rewarding. He was always a dynamic, enthusiastic, energetic show business professional, and he inspired everyone else to be as devoted to the craft as he was. It wasn't until the last few years of his career, when he was into his nineties, that his stamina and his performing precision began to falter.

One of the worst moments and one of the fondest memories of my joke-writing stint with Bob happened towards the end of his long and legendary career. He was preparing to tape a television monologue.

Bob's eyesight, which had troubled him for years, was getting worse and he was having trouble reading the cue cards. Barney Mc-Nulty, who prepared Bob's cue cards, made the letters about five inches tall and held them no more than five or six feet in front of him, but Bob still had trouble reading them.

I asked him once why he didn't wear glasses. I said, "Your audience will accept you in glasses. They did with Jack Benny."

Bob said, "Glasses don't do any good, Gene. It's like I'm looking at things in a smoke filled room. Glasses would just make the smoke clearer."

His reading of the monologue material became more and more halting. Struggling to see the cards threw his timing off noticeably.

At that particular monologue taping, I saw Bob in the dressing room before the show and mentioned to him that I had just heard on the radio that Johnny Carson, who had announced his retirement from *The Tonight Show,* was being honored by President George Bush, who was then a lame duck president. Bob hadn't heard about it.

The monologue went poorly. The audience was small. NBC claimed some of the buses bringing people to the taping were delayed or something. I suspected that NBC simply didn't attract a big audience because they were somewhat embarrassed by the latest Bob Hope specials.

Bob didn't deliver the material well because of the problems he had with his vision. The monologue didn't play well.

At the end of it, Bob called me up onstage. He covered the mike, leaned over to me and said, "Give me some jokes about Johnny Carson getting that honor."

I was surprised. I said, "When do you want them?"

He said, "Right now. I want to tell a few to the audience."

Miraculously, I immediately ad-libbed about five or six lines into Hope's ear. He stepped over to the microphone and recited them to the audience. Because he didn't have to read them, his timing was better, and because the topic was so current, the jokes played very well.

Bob said "Thank you and goodnight," and then he left to laughter and applause. It was the last television monologue he ever did.

Chapter Twenty-Two
Traveling with Bob Hope

Occasionally, Bob Hope took his specials on the road. Often, those were tie-ins with special events, like the show from New Orleans in 1984 while the World's Fair was in that city. Sometimes, they simply promoted tourism in various places like Tahiti, the Bahamas, Bermuda, Florida, Acapulco, and others.

My first traveling show with Bob was to London in 1978 to do a command performance at the Palladium in honor of the twenty-fifth

Conferring with Bob Hope during a taping of the All-American Football Team segment for a Christmas Special done in Florida.

anniversary of the coronation of Queen Elizabeth II. While there, I learned the true meaning of the saying "America and Great Britain are two countries separated by a common language." One day, while we were at a rehearsal at the Palladium, I was looking for Bob. I asked a few people where he was and they all gave me the same answer— "He's in the stalls." I kept searching because I had no idea where or what "the stalls" were. It turned out they were the seats right in the front of the stage.

Also, all of our jokes had to be "translated" by a British writer. What we called a "diaper" had to be changed to a "nappy."

We had several "nappy" jokes because the Queen had recently become a grandmother. At the rehearsal before the show, Bob was quickly rifling through the cue cards before his monologue. I sat beside him as he read. He came to one "nappy" joke and told Barney McNulty to throw it out. It was my joke. I said, "Bob, why are you throwing that out? It's a funny gag."

He said, "It's too rough to do for the Queen."

I said, "No, it's cute. The Queen will love that joke," I said, as if I knew what the Queen liked or disliked.

Hope said, "Do you really think so?"

I said, "Sure."

He handed me the card and said, "Then you do it."

He added, "Remember, she still has the power to behead."

He didn't do the joke.

There were a few others on that trip that he didn't do. For instance, one day he was rehearsing his monologue on stage and one of the gags, which I wrote, got some groans from the crew. Bob stopped the rehearsal, approached the front of the stage, and spoke to Bob Mills, another writer, and me. We were sitting in the first row of the theatre – in the stalls.

Bob asked me, "Is that your line?"

I meekly nodded yes.

He reached into his pocket, took out a bunch of keys, and threw them to Bob Mills. Mills caught them and asked, "What should I do with these?"

Bob said, "Take Perret to the Tower of London."

While those trips sounded appealing, there was very little time for tourism because the production always turned out to be a headache. Surprises presented themselves even when we did the shows from the Burbank studio, but there we coped with them more easily. All the equipment was available and within easy reach. On the road, we traveled with whatever equipment we thought we needed. If something unforeseen happened, which usually did, we had to adjust. It took more time, and consequently the schedule was thrown off. Shooting and rehearsing were out of whack.

The road shows were always more troublesome and more problematic than the studio shows. In Hawaii, the Judds were going to do a musical number at one of the major hotels. Since it was all music, I opted not to go to the taping. It was a wise decision because when I woke up the next morning, some of the crew members I saw were exhausted as they returned from the shoot. I discovered that every time they turned on the lights for the scene, they blew the power in the hotel. What should have taken an hour to tape, wound up taking the entire night.

In Pensacola, Florida, we were ready to shoot a sketch when we were hearing voices from people who weren't in our show. They were reading lines that we had never written. We discovered that radio waves were bouncing across the water from somewhere else in Florida and they were being transmitted over the wireless mikes that our performers were wearing.

At the New Orleans World's Fair special in May 1984, we had rain that cancelled a full day of taping and threw the schedule into turmoil. We were in the greatest city for food in the nation and we never got a chance to visit a restaurant. All our meals were sandwiches or po-boys sent to the rehearsal hall and we ate them from boxes. Often there were so many sandwiches packed into the delivered box that the ones on the bottom were flattened out and looked more like pizzas than sandwiches.

Also at that show, the outdoor stage was difficult to mike. The wireless mikes were picking up interference and the overhead mikes couldn't be used because we couldn't keep them out of the shot. Some of the writers offered suggestions that caused heated arguments. The sound guys didn't like suggestions coming from guys who just sat in the corner writing jokes.

As for me, I just sat in the corner writing jokes.

Several birthdays were celebrated on that show—Bob Hope, Brooke Shields, and I think either Marvin Hagler or Sugar Ray Leonard. For the finale, we planned to bring out a large birthday cake and celebrate all of them with the audience, but even that caused a problem.

The baker delivered the cake and then panicked. There was no way to keep the icing fresh until that segment of the show was being taped. Again, some writers offered suggestions which caused hard feelings.

As for me, I sat in the corner and wrote jokes.

I quickly learned that if there was a problem with the script, I had to work on it. If there was a problem anywhere else, the costumers, sound people, cameramen, technicians, bakers, or whomever, solved it much better than I, and they solved it without input from the guys who just sit in the corner and wrote jokes.

Once, I had a problem on a remote show that did require my input. It occurred even before we got to the location. The show was scheduled to be a command performance for King Gustav of Sweden. We had the first rehearsal at the Burbank studios before departing for Sweden.

The entire cast was there for the table reading, including Glen Campbell and Shirley Jones. During the script reading, Bob Hope turned to me at one point and said, "Gene, we could use a better line there."

I immediately ad-libbed a new line.

Bob said, "No."

I ad-libbed another. He rejected that one, too. I tried with a third line.

Bob said, "Gene, when we do a joke on my show, I like to have people know what the hell we're talking about."

Bob and I traded insults frequently, so I knew he was only kidding, but I went along with the gag. In front of the entire cast, I threw my pencil across the room, slammed my script to the floor, and shouted, "Bob, now you're getting into more expensive comedy."

It cracked Hope up and the rest of the cast, although stunned at first, joined in the laughter.

However, we may have had the ultimate complication on that road show. Many of the crew and some of the cast had flown ahead to Stockholm. Bob, the writers, and a few other staff people were scheduled to leave for Sweden late in the evening. We arrived at the airport and waited in the VIP lounge for our departure. While there, we had a few drinks, chatted, and watched television. Unexpectedly, we saw a shocking report that the Prime Minister of Sweden had just been assassinated. We had no idea what to do.

We wondered if the show would be cancelled because it involved the King and Queen. We were unsure whether or not to board our flight. We couldn't reach any of our people in Sweden to give us an opinion. A decision was finally made that we fly the eleven hours to Sweden, and if the show was cancelled or we weren't allowed in the country, then we'd simply get on another flight and fly right back to Los Angeles.

We got into the country, although security at the airport was very tight. The show went off without any further problems, other than the ones we either brought with us or caused while we were there.

Although the work schedule was always tough on those trips, we did have our share of laughs, too. Bob's crew made great traveling companions, and Bob, an old vaudevillian, was great fun on those jaunts.

Once, a few of us sat in Bob's suite going over some changes in the script. While we were working, Dolores Hope, his wife, came in to say goodbye to him before she headed off on a shopping spree. Just as she got to the door, Bob called after her, "Remember, don't buy anything here that you can get at K-Mart."

We traveled in style, at least the writers did. Guild rules demanded that we travel first class, so the rooms were always pleasant. We partied constantly because whoever was hosting the trip always had some sort of shindig for Bob and his troupe.

Bob's crew and staff were delightful. We had our disagreements in the midst of production, but no one carried that over to the social aspects of the trip. However, one of our constant goals while traveling was to get the other folks jealous. During a discussion, I casually mentioned that the Jacuzzi in my room wasn't delivering enough hot water. Of course, I had no Jacuzzi in my room, but everyone else on the trip wondered if I did. Folks were constantly referring to the living room in their suite, or the balcony overlooking a great view. We just liked to torment one another about our mythical accommodations.

Bob stayed in the best suite at hotels, and it was nice to spend so much time in such luxurious surroundings. When I and a few of my fellow travelers first visited one of Bob's magnificent suites, I might have gotten in the ultimate one-upsmanship He took us on a tour of the place because even he was impressed with it.

During the tour I said, "This is just like my room except my kitchen and dining room are on the other side of the suite from yours."

Those traveling shows were a lot of work for the writers even though the scripts were written before we left home. First of all, there were usually only one or two writers on those jaunts. So, those two did the work that ten or twelve would be doing at home. Of course, the writers who stayed home were only a phone call away, but normally, it was easier to work on the script and get the changes made rather than call the other writers and have them call in their work.

There was so much rewriting to do on one show that we did from Hawaii that Bob Mills and I were practically prisoners in our room. We rushed to get the final sketch done in time for taping so we could wrap the show and make our flights home. We typed a page or two and a runner picked those pages up, copied them, and got them into the script. Then, he returned for the next couple of pages. We finished up the final pages and went down to watch the sketch we had just written being rehearsed and taped.

During that same show, we hurried to write a talk spot for Loni Anderson and Bob. Loni had appeared in a movie of the week that did well in the ratings the previous night. It was about a woman who became a hooker to provide for her daughter and herself. Since it made such a splash in the press, we did some lines about it in the talk spot.

Bob Hope was taping a talk spot with Tom Selleck on the set of *Magnum P.I.* While he was away, we got word from the producers that Loni was furious with the new pages. Normally, Hope would handle problems like those, but that time, Bob Mills and I had to handle it.

We had worked with Loni many times before on the Bob Hope specials. She was always pleasant to work with, knew her lines, and could handle comedy well, but I suppose us trivializing the successful show that was broadcast the previous night had upset her.

Loni was quite angry when we went to her suite. She told us in no uncertain terms that she thought the material was distasteful and filthy.

I asked, "Which lines do you object to?"

She said, "All of them."

I used a device that served me well when I worked at General Electric. I asked if we could go through the piece line by line and isolate the offensive ones. Loni agreed.

We started with Hope saying, "Hello, Loni." Then I asked, "Now do you have an objection to that?"

She said, "Of course not."

Then we moved on to Loni replying, "Hi, Bob, good to see you."

"Any objection to that response?"

"Of course not."

We went through the entire talk spot that way. Any line that Loni thought was questionable, we immediately removed. We wound up cutting only a small portion of the routine and we still had plenty left to do on the show.

It was the last thing to be shot and Loni did do it, although she still wasn't too happy about it. It played well, though.

Bob Mills and I were a bit worried that Hope might have felt that we mishandled the situation. On the contrary, he was pleased with what we did. In fact, he was a little bit upset that Loni had called from Hawaii to speak with her agent in Los Angeles. She asked him to talk to Bob's representative in Los Angeles, who in turn, called the show in Hawaii. He figured she could have just as easily called his room, or stopped down to discuss the material.

That evening, after the piece was taped, Bob Mills and I sat at the outside bar in the hotel breezeway. We saw Bob Hope come down and walk by the bar on his way to the limousines. As he did, he was mobbed by fans wanting photos with him and autographs. He was gracious to all of them. Then, he got in his black limo and drove off.

A few moments later, Loni came down and walked the same route. Fans were eager for photos and autographs, but she was still annoyed and looked straight ahead, ignoring all of the fans. Mills and I watched that procession from our seats at the nearby bar.

Loni got into her beautiful white stretch limo without ever acknowledging the crowd. The driver closed her door and then got into the driver's seat. We listened as he tried to start the engine, but it wouldn't turn over. He tried again.

Eventually, he got out, opened the door for Loni, and they switched to a lowly black limo and drove off. Mills enjoyed that spectacle so much that he bought a round of drinks for the others at the bar.

Sometimes, the location itself caused changes when a set wasn't as the writers envisioned it, so new lines were hurriedly needed. We also rehearsed on the location, so changes sometimes sprang naturally from that. Cast members sometimes wanted new lines, a director suggested changes, and so on.

Bob Hope always wanted new lines for the script, regardless of how well rehearsals were going. We once had a late night rehearsal in the hotel room and the sketch played like dynamite. It got big laughs and everyone in the cast loved it. It was magnificent, but at the end of the rehearsal, Bob caught my eye and motioned me over.

He said, "Come on up to my room after rehearsal."

I asked, "Why?"

He said, "We can make this better."

I said, "It was brilliant."

He said, "So. We'll work on it for awhile. If we make it better, it'll be better. If we don't, it'll still be brilliant."

We worked on changes for that fantastic sketch. I suppose we made it a little better.

Bob was also one of the problems for those location shows in other ways, too. He was a major star. He could disrupt production if he wanted to. One morning, I sat with him in his suite before a scheduled shooting. We were due on the set, but Bob didn't seem to be worried by that.

He said to me, "What time do we have to be down there?"

I said, "They wanted to shoot at ten o'clock." It was then about ten minutes after ten.

He said, "Oh, boy, we'd better get a move on. Do you want some breakfast?"

He got on the phone and ordered breakfast to be sent up. We ate and then went down to the set. Of course, Bob was also paying for all of that, so once he finally got on the set, he acted upset that we were running behind. "Let's go, let's go," he'd say impatiently. "This is costing me money."

On one special, we had completed all the taping except for the "tribute." The tribute was the ending of the shows where Bob said a few inspiring words and then sang a short, special lyric version of "Thanks for the Memory." We were going to shoot that early the next morning, and then head to the airport for the journey home.

That evening, Bob, producer Eliot Kozak, and I went out on Bob's veranda that had a view of the entire complex and beach. We planned out the locations for the various tribute segments. At first, Bob was to stroll along the beach. Then, we were to cut to the waterfall in the hotel garden, and then we were to go somewhere else. It was all discussed and decided on.

The following morning, Bob showed up on the beach location and said, "What are we shooting here for? We have a beach in Los Angeles." We had to break down all the setups and relocate. It took a bit of time and our flights were delayed.

In Tahiti, we had an early morning production meeting in the living room of Bob's suite. We were discussing locations and trying to plan the shooting schedule for that day. People offered suggestions and Bob wouldn't hear them. His hearing was failing a bit at the time and it was difficult to get our ideas heard.

Finally, we got our day planned out and the crew began to exit to get their work started. Two guys were just about at the doorway, a long way from Bob, when one whispered, "I don't get paid enough money to put up with this sort of nonsense."

Bob immediately hollered to them, "You get paid plenty."

Either he heard everything we said during the meeting and purposely ignored some of it, or he only heard sentences that had the word "money" in them. We didn't know.

Normally, as a writer, I traveled "above the line." That means I was considered part of the talent and that my expenses were covered. I never had to settle a room bill or pay for any of my meals. While the crew often had to settle for phone calls made on their room bills, I didn't. I simply went and all traveling expenses were on the company, until one of the writers began abusing the privilege. My philosophy was that I would treat myself the way I would normally treat myself at home. If I wanted a steak, I'd have a steak. If I wanted a glass of wine with that steak, I'd order a reasonable wine. I didn't put any extras on my tab.

Sometimes, the writers bought wine for the entire table or bought shirts from the resort and billed them to the room. Rather than a reasonably priced wine, they'd order the more expensive vintages.

Bob found out about that and ordered that the writers would henceforth be put on a per diem. We'd get a certain amount for travel expenses, and from that, we'd have to pay for our own room, meals, and so on.

I was upset with that—what I considered a demotion. On the very first trip under the new plan, I got my per diem in cash and wound up when the trip was over with an extra $400 in my pocket. I never spent as much as the per diem.

Nevertheless, my ego longed for the status of traveling "above the line."

Despite being a lot of work for the writers, the traveling shows were fun. Hope surrounded himself with enjoyable people and working with them was usually a delight.

On our flight to Tahiti, our crew had the entire first class section of a 747. It was about a fourteen-hour flight and it started out to be a flying party. After meals were served, everyone was ready for a nap and we all settled back, but then we heard a sound like a voice crackling over a radio or something. It started with static sounds and then a barely discernible voice. We all listened.

Then, it happened again. Still, we couldn't make out what was being said, but then we did hear the voice. It began with static, and then we heard, "Enemy aircraft approaching at eleven o'clock."

We all popped up and looked out the windows to see what was happening. It turned out to be Jonathan Winters, with that incredibly talented voice of his, having some fun with us.

Jonathan was also responsible for one of the funniest moments I've ever enjoyed in show business. In Tahiti, someone threw a part for us almost every evening. The food was always the same—typical island buffet dishes, and the music was always ukuleles played by grass-skirted natives.

After about five nights of that, we were all at a buffet where Bob and Jonathan sat at the head table with the writers and a few others at a table next to that. We had the same food, and an island band played throughout the meal. Jonathan got up to stretch his legs, came over to us writers, knelt down, put his arms around two of us, and then said, "I don't know about you boys, but musically, this is the most exciting evening of my life."

I could not stop laughing. Hope called me over and asked what Jonathan said, but since he was sitting next to our host, I had to make something up. Of course, I told him later.

One of my other favorite moments happened while we were doing a show in the Bahamas. Hope was shooting a scene with Barbara Mandrell in the main square of Nassau. After the taping, we were headed back to our hotel. There were four of us in the limousine, including Bob, Bob's makeup man, who had a large moustache, me with a bald head and full beard, and the driver, a six-foot, eight-inch muscle-bound guy, who was as much bodyguard as he was chauffeur. Traffic was heavy through the main market place, and at one time, we came to a dead halt. Bob put the back window down for some air.

A very heavy native woman, who was selling woven hats, came over to our limo, put her head into the car, and was nose to nose with Bob. She looked at him for a while, glanced at me sitting next to him, looked at the driver, and then looked at the makeup man in the passenger seat. She smiled, and then went back around, glancing at all of us again. Finally, she asked, "Okay, which one is Bob Hope?"

There wasn't a sound from any of us in the car. Eventually, Bob put up the window and we got moving again. About a block away, Bob said, "Which one is Bob Hope?" and we all took a fit of laughing.

I got one of my biggest and most memorable laughs when we were rehearsing for a show in Pope Air Force Base in Fayetteville, North Carolina. Lucille Ball was a guest on that show and one of the pieces had to do with reincarnation. In the sketch, Bob had a joke about what Lucy was some 200 years ago.

During a break in the rehearsal, Lucille called me over and said, "I want a comeback to Bob's joke. I want to say something funny about him 200 years ago. What could Bob Hope have been 200 years ago?"

I said, "Bob Hope."

Lucy literally fell off her chair and started slapping the ground. The joke stayed in the show and got big laughs.

While we were taping that show, President Reagan called and said he would stop in on his flight home from Alabama and be on the show since it was honoring our fighting men.

We had just received that call when the entire compound was suddenly overrun with Secret Service men in uniforms and suits, accompanied by bomb-sniffing dogs. Hope told Bob Mills and me to write "a little vaudeville bit for me and the Prez."

We wrote about three or four pages of gags for Hope and Reagan. Bob read them over and said, "Come with me."

We went to a large trailer on the compound where the Secret Service headquartered. From there, we called Air Force One, which was en route to our show.

We rehearsed the bit on the phone with the President. He suggested a few changes and we incorporated them into the bit.

A little while later, Air Force One landed on the strip at Pope AFB, just a few hundred yards from our stage. A limousine drove the President to the stage. He went over the cue cards with Bob, and then he taped the segment in front of the troops. Afterwards, he headed back to whatever work was waiting for him in Washington. His appearance was quite exciting.

I also got a little insight into Hollywood personalities, too. While we were writing that piece, Gary Morton, Lucille's husband, was in the trailer with Bob Mills and me. We knew the President was on his way, but that was about all. While we were writing, Gary was on the phone with one of his pals in Hollywood, and we heard him say, "Yeah, I've been kind of busy. Lucy and I spent the whole day with the President . . . ."

Those jaunts were exhausting for our cast, crew, and writers, but Hope seemed to thrive on those trips. He stayed lively and energetic. Maybe he had better accommodations and more rest, or maybe it was because he forged his career in vaudeville, which was constant travel and work. His biography wasn't titled "Have Tux, Will Travel" for nothing.

Our exit from Tahiti was quite confused. We left Moorea in the rain and journeyed to the airport in Papeete, only to discover that there was no plane for us. We went to a hotel on Papeete with assurances that we would be called back to the airport within a few hours. We stayed overnight.

Our luggage had been transported to the airport, so our stay at the hotel was a bit uncomfortable because we had no toiletries or change of clothing.

The next morning, we were again told to be ready to go the airport on a moment's notice, but no notice ever came. We stayed another uncomfortable night at the hotel in Papeete. Bob and Dolores Hope were not traveling home with us from Tahiti. They were going on to the Orient, so they were unaware of our flight problems. Finally, after another uncomfortable evening at the Papeete hotel, we got a call the next day to go to the airport. Ticket counters at the Papeete airport are all outdoors. We stood in line in the tropical sun for over two hours.

The airline we were originally booked on had no planes available because of a minor accident in Australia, or some such story. We were being rebooked on United Airlines, but we could not get boarding passes until our tickets were paid for in cash. That was the reason for our delay at the airport.

In any case, we were tired from spending two days at the hotel waiting for word and standing for over two hours in the sun waiting for our boarding passes. While we were in line, Bob's limousine pulled up to the airport. He was ready to board his flight to the Orient. As he walked by, he approached Bob Mills and me standing in line.

He said, "Start thinking about the next show."

Chapter Twenty-Three
Going to War with Bob Hope

Once, Don Rickles was taping a special for television and Bob Hope walked into the theatre. Rickles stopped his routine and shouted to Bob, "Who's minding the war?"

Bob first began entertaining the military with a trip to March Air Force Base in California in 1941. Eventually, during World War II, he traveled to the spots where the battles were being fought and that became a tradition of his until he retired from performing in the late 1990's. During the Vietnam era, Bob's Christmas specials with the troops were eagerly anticipated and among the highest rated shows of all time.

I wrote for several of Bob's Vietnam shows, but I never accompanied him on those jaunts. I was always working on other shows and couldn't get the time off. Bob, though, sent me information on the various bases he visited and I wrote jokes for all of them. I also wrote generic lines such as:

"It's so hot here . . . ."

"It's so cold here . . . ."

"It's so muddy here . . . ."

"It's so dry here . . . ."

A few years later, Mort Lachman, who was Bob's producer and head-writer for the Vietnam trips, told me how much of a problem my lines generated. I asked why, and he explained that the cue cards that the troupe carried were a major logistic problem. Bob had a different routine for each base and the collection of cards filled a couple of trucks. They tried to separate them by the different camps they were visiting so that they wouldn't have to load and unload the entire accumulation of cards each time. However, Bob often asked, "Where are the 'mud' jokes?" "Find me the 'heat' jokes," or whatever. Then, they'd have to go through the entire collection of jokes to find the 'generic' routine of mine that Bob wanted to include.

In 1983, Bob was going to journey to the battlefields again to visit the troops in Beirut, Lebanon. That was a different kind of trip because it was based at sea. All of his other military travels were on land. Being at sea limited the number of personnel that could accompany him.

Eliot Kozak, who was producing the shows then, asked me if I wanted to go. The area was quite volatile at the time, so my first reaction was to say, "No," and I did, but I immediately regretted my reply. I had begun my career by studying Bob's comedy style. I had become a major contributor to his writing staff and part of the Bob Hope legend. Then, I had a chance to see him in the arena that was to be his hallmark—entertaining troops in the battle areas, so I went back to Kozak and said, "I'll go. I want to go."

However, no one was sure if there would be room enough for a writer on that jaunt, so I wasn't at all sure I would be with the troupe when they departed on the following Tuesday morning.

On Sunday evening, we taped our regularly scheduled Christmas

This is me preparing to board our DC-9 to begin our journey to New York, and then on to the Mediterranean to entertain our troops fighting in Beirut, Lebanon.

special at NBC studios in Burbank. After the taping several of us writers were in Bob Hope's dressing room. Hope dressed and was getting ready to go home. As he passed me in the doorway, he whispered, "Pack."

I was on the plane on Tuesday.

We began that trip on a Navy DC-9, which was arranged just like a normal passenger airliner. In the forward part of the craft, there were four bunk beds, and behind that were the first class seats, which were two sets of seats on each side of the aisle facing each other with a table between them. Then, there were partitions separating the first class from rows of seats in the tourist section. I was assigned the second aisle seat in the tourist section on the left hand side of the aircraft.

My seatmate, whom I'd never met before, was Dale Hostetler,

Bob's masseur. We introduced ourselves, made some small talk, and then settled down for the long journey to Beirut.

Bob was in the first class section on the same side of the aircraft as I was. The first class partition was between us. However, during the flight, he moved over to the other side of the aircraft. I got up and moved over to the other side, also. Later, Bob moved back across the aisle. I did, too.

Bob moved several times during the flight. Each time he moved, I moved. Finally, Dale asked me, "What are you doing moving back and forth across the aisle so much?" I explained to him that I always wanted the partition between me and Bob. "If he catches my eye," I told Dale, "I'll have to go to work writing jokes."

While I was explaining that to Dale, Bob moved across the aisle again. When I turned, he was looking directly at me. Our eyes met and he motioned for me to come see him. He wanted material. He moved up to where the bunk beds were and laid down in one as he explained what he needed. I sat on the bed across the aisle, taking notes.

"We'll be landing in New Jersey and they'll have a press conference there," he said. "I'll need some gags."

"Okay," I said.

"Maybe we can do some things about bringing the beautiful . . . ."

He stopped. I glanced at him and saw that he was enjoying a nap. I lay down for a bit of a rest, too, but I didn't sleep.   About ten minutes later, Bob woke up and immediately continued, ". . . girls to the troops." He had taken a short nap in mid-sentence.

The Navy was pleased to have us on their DC-9. The chef on the flight, so we heard, was from the White House. However, Bob wasn't satisfied with the accommodations. The craft was comfortable enough, and the treatment we received was gracious, but the DC-9 had to stop for refueling several times on the way to the Mediterranean. That, of course, made for a much longer flight.

So, Bob contacted Casper Weinberger, then Secretary of State, and arranged for us to transfer to a C-141 transport craft when we stopped on the East Coast. That plane could be refueled in the air and could get us to Oman without stopping.

The new craft had rows of seats bolted down for our crew, but it also had two VIP compartments. Those were like mobile homes that could be rolled onto the craft and bolted down. They were quite comfortable with large seats, couches, desks, and so on. Since we'd be doing a lot of rehearsing during the flight, I was assigned a seat in the VIP lounges along with the cast.

It was much more comfortable. The only real discomfort was that Cathy Lee Crosby had a cassette of her song numbers. She put on a headset, so she was the only one who could hear the musical accompaniment, but she sang full out for a goodly portion of the flight.

We landed in Oman and then transferred to helicopters to deliver us to the *USS Guam*, a helicopter carrier that would be our home and headquarters for the duration of our trip. When I was thinking about the trip, I pictured myself flying around in the type of helicopters they used for traffic reports on local radio. I visualized me and one or two other passengers buzzing around over the Mediterranean. The helicopter we boarded was a biggie, large enough to take all forty or so of the troupe along with all of our equipment.

We were all issued life vests and helmets with earmuffs to cut down on the noise. We had to wear them. I must have looked terrified because Bob glanced at me and laughed. He pulled away one of my earmuffs and said, "You look like the company Rabbi."

I really wasn't too concerned until one Marine stood up front to give us our safety instructions. He showed us how to hook up the seat belts, which were a bit more complicated than the normal passenger airline belts. Then, he issued the instructions in a gruff, Marine drill instructor tone.

He said, "Should we crash at sea . . . ."

I turned to Bob and mouthed the word, "crash?"

The marine continued. ". . . wait until all violent motion ceases . . . ."

I turned to Bob and mouthed, "violent motion?"

". . . then evacuate the aircraft and gather at the front of the craft. Should we crash on land . . . ."

Again, I mouthed the word to Bob.

". . . wait until all violent motion ceases . . . ."

I did it again.

". . . then evacuate the aircraft and gather at the front of the craft."

I looked towards Bob as if to say, "What have you gotten me into?"

He lifted my ear covering again and said, "You're probably not going to get a bag of peanuts on this flight, either."

It was a breathtaking experience when we landed on the USS Guam. First of all, it was exciting to look down and see that tiny speck in the Mediterranean and realize that was where we were going to land.

When we did settle on the deck and disembark, there were servicemen and women all over the place. They were hanging from the railings and climbing up on any piece of equipment that would hold them. It was amazing.

Bob was greeted by the brass, of course. As they walked along, I followed, but I kept looking around at the wall of sailors that were waving to us. Finally, when I turned to follow our group, they were gone. One minute, they were standing behind me, and the next minute, they had disappeared. They literally disappeared.

I had no idea where they went.

A young sailor saw my confusion and rescued me. "They went down on the elevator," he said. I didn't know it, but they have a large elevator on the side of the ship that takes aircraft up and down from the hanger deck to the flight deck. I was late stepping onto it and it went down without me. That sailor offered to help me meet up with the rest of the troupe, and then he offered to take me on a tour of the ship. I went along gladly.

He led me through the guts of the ship. I had no idea where I was going or how to get back to anyplace. At one point, he took me outside on a lower deck. It was just a small terrace, but while we were there, some helicopters were coming in for a landing. I asked if I could take some pictures. He said, "You don't have a flash on, do you?"

I told him I didn't.

He said it would be okay, then. The flash, though, might blind the pilots momentarily and cause a disaster.

I took the photos without the flash. When I turned to talk to my escort again, he was gone. That time, he had literally disappeared.

When he reappeared a minute or two later, I asked where he went. He told me he liked to be inside when the choppers come in. "Many times," he warned me, "they will miss and crash into the side of the ship."

That was great news because our schedule called for us to be flying around in those things for the next ten days or so.

Then, that young sailor took me inside the ship and was very proud that the *USS Guam* had the only photo development lab in the fleet. He took me in to see it. There was a large photo dryer, a tumbler, almost like the cages that you see when they roll cards around for a random prize drawing. Inside it were hundreds of photos that had been developed in the lab and were being dried. He took a few out and showed them to me. They were all photos of crashed and mangled helicopters, the very craft that I was to be flying around in for the next ten days.

The sailor boasted that the ship also had a "7-11" on board. "Would you like to see it?"

I told him, "Of course, I would."

As he was leading me, I thought that I'd be seeing a large area on the ship that housed a secret weapon, the "7-11," whatever that was. I thought it would be a sleek plane or a fancy rocket ship, or something like that.

When we arrived, he pointed proudly and said, "There it is."

It was a small cubby hole of a store that sold candy, film, toothpaste, razors, or whatever. It was a 7-ll store.

Our first show was that evening. Frankly, I was not enthused. I was afraid that Bob might be out of his element. He served well in World War II, Korea, and Viet Nam, but I thought that the new generation might not be impressed. Boy, was I wrong. The show was in the hanger deck of the Guam, and again, military personnel crowded the floor and also hung from every perch imaginable, and what an audience they were. Bob's monologue played beautifully. Everything we did in the show was a smash. The military loved him and the feeling was mutual.

Working on the Mediterranean was difficult because all our travel

**These were the kinds of crowds that turned out
for every show we did for the Military.**

was by helicopter. We did all of the shows on various ships in the
fleet. Consequently, we had to get up early in the morning—usually
around 6:00 a.m.—in order to make the trip. We flew with our crew
and equipment to whatever ships we were working on that day.

Bob was not a morning person; he didn't want to wake early. He
said, "Fly the equipment there, set up the stage, and then I'll fly in for
the show."

The Navy said, "You can't."

Bob asked, "Why not?"

They explained, "Once we set up the stage on the deck of the ship,
there's no place to land a helicopter."

We all had to go to the ship, have the crew set up for the show, do

**Bob Hope hamming it up with Brooke Shields
on one of our chopper flights near Beirut.**

the show, and then break down the set, gather the equipment, load it on the helicopter, and fly back to the Guam. Those were long days.

Bob kept me writing, though. On one flight, I was seated on the chopper across the aisle from where he was sitting next to Vic Damone. Bob motioned for me to come over. I went over, but I could hardly hear him because of the noise of the helicopter. He grabbed my writing pad and pencil and jotted down, "Get a new line for Vic. The one he has now isn't working."

I jotted a note and handed the pad back to Bob. It read, "All <u>my</u> jokes are working."

He took the pad from me and wrote, "You're lucky you are."

Then, I wrote a gag on the pad and handed it back. He nodded "no."

I tried another and handed it across the aisle. Again, it was rejected.

We did this a few more times. Finally, Bob asked for the pad and pencil. He wrote a note and handed it back to me. It read, "Forget it. Why are we busting our ass to make him a star?"

Bob and I laughed and Vic Damone sat there completely oblivious to what was going on.

As the only writer on the trip, Bob wanted me with the cast wherever they went. We might do some last minute rehearsing or make some quick script changes. It was humbling at times, especially when we visited the other ships. When our helicopter landed on the deck of a ship, there were always hundreds of sailors and marines waiting for the doors to open so they could see Bob, George Kirby, Vic Damone, Cathy Lee Crosby, Ann Jillian, Miss USA, Brooke Shields, and me.

Guess which one didn't get mobbed.

I almost got pushed overboard several times in their rush to get to the girls for autographs and pictures.

On the flight over, the USO gave all of us on the trip white satin tennis jackets. They had an emblem on the breast and a giant caricature of Bob Hope on the back with "Bob Hope USO Tour—7th Fleet—Beirut, Lebanon" in red, white, and blue letters. I wore it everywhere because it identified me as part of the troupe and not military personnel.

One day, the cast was going to do a show that wasn't being televised, so I didn't have to go with them. I waited on the deck of the USS New Jersey for the next helicopter back to the Guam. While I was waiting, a young marine, who was going to go back to the fighting in Beirut, came over to me and asked, "Can I have my picture taken with you?"

I was thrilled. I said, "Sure you can. That's why we're here."

He said, "Let me show my buddy how to operate the camera."

He told another marine how to snap the photo. When he came back to me, I put my arm around his shoulder and gave him a big smile.

He said, "No, no, no, man. Turn around."

All he wanted was the back of my jacket.

On another day, Bob was late getting up to the deck after a show. The Navy told us that they would absolutely not fly the helicopters after dark because it was too dangerous. So while the performers and I waited for Bob to arrive, the helicopter took off without us.

The captain of the ship offered two suggestions: we could stay on-board overnight, or he would get a small craft to bring us back to the Guam. We couldn't stay overnight because we had an early departure the next morning for that day's show. We had to make the two-hour journey by boat. The sea was rough that night, and they had no running lights because they made too great a target on the open sea. The Mediterranean water looked pitch black. It was a rough journey.

The trip was even rougher when we got to the Guam. We docked next to a floating dock outside the ship. The waves were at least four-feet high, so at any one time, the dock and our boat could have been as much as eight-feet away from one another. They had several sailors helping us make the jump from boat to dock and then up the outside of the carrier. I was concerned about the cast, but they all made it safely.

The last two people to make the transition were Bob and me. Bob didn't seem concerned. He just hummed, and when his turn came, he stepped forward and the seas calmed. It was almost Biblical. The seas ceased their turmoil and he walked casually across.

When I got there, the water raged again. Mercifully, the sailors guided me safely across. When I reached the innards of the ship, a sailor greeted me. He had a large poster of his ship, the *USS Guam*. He had gotten every cast member to sign it. He asked me, the last one off, if I would sign it, too.

Again, I said, "Sure. That's why we're here."

As I was preparing to sign it, he said, "What do you do on the show?"

I said proudly, "I'm the writer."

He hesitated, and then said, "Sign it anyway."

The logistics on that show were problematic. All of the equipment had to be transported back and forth with each show. Cue cards especially were a burden. They had to be organized, tied up, and then lugged from the helicopter landing pad to wherever the show was being performed. Bob also wanted them available for rehearsal, so they often had to be packaged and carried up or down several decks before each show and then back to the show venue.

Our last show of that tour was on the aircraft carrier, *USS John F. Kennedy*. While the costumes were being hauled aboard, they simply disappeared. They were unloaded onto the ship, but they never reached the stage. The ship's personnel hunted for them, but they couldn't locate them.

We had no costumes for the numbers or for the sketches. Brooke Shields came up with a very workable idea. The girls borrowed military jackets from the officers onboard and wore them over their leotards. The makeshift costumes looked quite becoming and very sexy. They were used for the final cut of the show that aired on NBC.

I made every military jaunt with Bob after that 1983 trip to Beirut.

We traveled to the Persian Gulf a couple of times. We did a Peace Time jaunt around the world in 1989. It was supposed to be Bob's farewell to the military, however, as we were coming home, trouble began brewing in Kuwait. When we landed home, Bob said to me, "Don't unpack."

We were on our way to Saudi Arabia less than a month later.

It was a strange melding of attitudes and personalities when the Bob Hope troupes visited service bases. The military was all discipline and leadership, yet nothing seemed to get done. Our gang was ragtag, haphazard, seemingly aimless, yet the shows got on the stage and on the air quite well.

The disparity was very apparent during our trip to Beirut. One marine gentleman traveling with us was a weekend warrior and an executive at NBC. He prided himself on his military bearing. He could just about tolerate our crew of ruffians.

One day after the show was done and the set was dismantled, we were all milling about waiting for our helicopter to go back to our ship. We were chatting away, laughing, and having a good time. That irritated him. He wanted marine-like discipline. Finally, he took matters into his own hands. While we were jawing away, he climbed up onto a box and shouted in a powerful voice, "I want your full attention, please."

Our babble stopped immediately.

He bellowed, "I want the following people to report to me, front and center, on the double." Then, he shouted out a bunch of names from our cast.

When he was done, we all turned and resumed our chit-chat. No one reported to him *on the double* or anyway else. He slunk down from his soapbox and withdrew. We didn't see much of him for the rest of the trip.

Everyone on those trips had a job to do, including writing, lighting, sound, cameras, and makeup. Whatever they were, the folks did them well. It was an efficient show-producing squad. However, the main job of the troupe was gathering souvenirs. We all tried to get hats, jackets, patches, ashtrays, cigarette lighters, or whatever they were offering.

Once, though, I wanted to abandon one guy who was souvenir hunting. We had landed in Bahrain and it was unnerving to me. The marines who flew us in were a bit apprehensive about our visit there, and I was even more so. When we got off the C-141, people surrounded us with automatic weapons. They were non-English speaking foreign soldiers. I didn't know whether they were protecting us from harm or waiting for us to make a false move so they could cause us harm. We were dispatched in small groups to helicopters. I kept hoping that my name would be called quickly so that I could get away from those guys. However, others kept going before me. Finally, I was in the last group of about eight people, so I knew I had to be on the next chopper.

An American marine was dispatching us and giving us our instructions. I just wanted him to talk quickly so we could move out to the landing area, board our helicopter, and be on our way.

Just as we were about to leave, one of our group commented on the patch the marine wore. "Can I get one of those?" he asked.

"Sure," the marine said, "Wait here and I'll go get some."

Our marine left and I was sentenced to an even longer wait surrounded by those guys with the automatic guns. However, I did get a nice patch.

Bahrain caused me other heartaches, too. It was a fascinating place, known as the Las Vegas of the Middle East, but it was dangerous because its borders were so open. It was ripe for terrorists, and the Bob Hope troupes were attractive targets for thugs. The military were concerned about us during any visits there. During "Desert Shield," we were advised not to leave our hotel without armed escorts.

During one visit to Bahrain, we went on a shopping spree. Bob was accompanied by the Commodore, and I was a few steps behind him with the Captain of our ship. I noticed the Captain was uncomfortable in Bahrain, so again, I was even more so.

People from the military had warned us to be on our good behavior. We weren't to take any pictures of people if they didn't want them taken. We weren't to do anything illegal. The stories had it that they cut off fingers or hands for thievery.

During our shopping tour, I had to go to the bathroom, but I couldn't locate a men's room. Not many people spoke English, so I had trouble asking. The situation was becoming critical. I wondered if they cut off hands for stealing, what they cut off for urinating in the promenade. Finally, I saw a door that seemed to be a men's rest room. I went to it and found it was locked. I jiggled the door a bit, figuring maybe it was only stuck. When I turned around, an armed guard had a gun pointed at my nose. He marched me down to a nearby store, spoke to the clerk, and he handed me a key to the men's room. It didn't matter. After the gun incident, I didn't have to go any more.

During our walk through the shopping center, we lost Bob and the Commodore. We were scheduled to go to a party at the U.S. Ambassador's house that evening, so I suggested to the Captain that we get our driver and go right to the party. The Captain didn't know where the Ambassador's house was. He didn't know where our driver was, either. Fortunately, our driver, who was probably more bodyguard than driver, knew where we were. He drove us to the Ambassador's house and we enjoyed a very elegant party. Nevertheless, I wanted to leave.

After the party, I was in the first car to the waiting C-141. Bob was already on board. As I passed him, he called me over. "How'd you like that palace, huh?"

I said, "It was gorgeous."

"And a nice party, too," Bob said.

I said, "Yeah, it was great. There was only one problem."

"What's that?" Bob asked.

Behind my back I pulled my hand up into the sleeve of my jacket. I held the "handless" sleeve out to Bob and said, "You steal one lousy ashtray."

Bob fell out of his seat and started banging his hand on the floor laughing. It was the biggest reaction I ever got from the boss.

On many of those trips, we moved around quickly and did several shows a day. We also crossed over time zones. The rules of thumb were that if someone gave us something to eat, we ate it; if we had a chance to sleep, we took it.

We were never sure how much sleep we would get. We had a lot of work to do and we were always on a tight schedule, but we also were never sure what sort of sleeping arrangements we'd have. One night, we had a luxurious, comfortable room. The next night, we had a cot, and sometimes, not even that.

Even when we had comfortable accommodations, we couldn't

count on a good night's sleep. In Berlin, I was quartered in a three-room suite that was reserved for generals. It was beautiful. It had a lovely shower stall and a complimentary bar. I showered, had a cocktail or two, and then settled down in a most comfortable bed for a solid evening of rest. At two o'clock, the phone rang. It was Mrs. Hope. She was watching the Kentucky Derby, which because of the time difference, aired at that hour in Berlin, and she wanted to know if I was watching it.

"No," I said.

"Well you just won it," she said. That year, a jockey named Craig Perret was astride the winning horse. It was good fortune for Craig Perret, but bad fortune for Gene Perret. I never did get back to sleep that night.

Coming back from Beirut, the base served us breakfast before we left at about three o'clock in the morning. On the plane, the cooks prepared some scrambled eggs and bacon for us. When we landed at Lajes Field in the Azores, they had breakfast waiting for us. Our first stop after that was Fort Dix in New Jersey, where they had breakfast planned for us. We had four breakfasts on our way home.

On one trip, I sat in the body of the C-141 because the VIP section on that craft was tiny. My seatmate was a hardworking soul, who did the publicity for the tour. He was constantly writing on his laptop and rushing out to have the copy sent by whatever means to wherever he sent it. I know he was doing a bang-up job, but he was also a pest as far as I was concerned. Every time I dozed off, he'd wake me up by climbing over me. I wasn't getting much rest at all.

On our flight home, our roles were reversed. All his publicity work was done, but I still had writing to do for radio shows and interviews that Bob was to perform wherever we stopped.

That gentleman rolled up in several blankets and went sound asleep, and he stayed asleep for a long time. I sat on the aisle, he was by the wall, and there was an empty seat between us. At one point, he and his blankets fell over onto the empty seat. I couldn't see his face because of the blankets and I couldn't see if he was breathing. I thought he had died.

I wanted to pull the blankets away and see if he was alive. Then I thought that because he had worked hard on that trip, he deserved his rest. If he was deceased, there was no helping him, and if he was alive but asleep, he should just sleep. He woke, eventually.

Most of the trip was party time . . . and work. It wasn't easy to mount a show in arenas like those. We worked hard, but we also shared a lot of laughs. We did have a few harrowing experiences, though. After all, there was fighting going on.

Strangely enough, my most traumatic experience was during our Peacetime trip around the world. We visited Moscow. The people of Russia were delightful, but the folks in authority were very militant. The clerks at the hotel didn't say, "Have a nice day." They said very authoritatively, "Stand in this line and have your documents ready."

I was pleased to have visited Moscow, but eager to get out again. Our military escorts instructed us, on our departure, to board the C-141. They told us our passports, which had been collected by the Soviet authorities upon our arrival, would be handed out once we were in the air. So, we obediently took our assigned seats on the plane. We taxied out to the runway for take-off. Then, we stopped. The Russian militia boarded and ordered all of us off the plane and instructed us to stand in front of it. Only Dolores and Bob were exceptions. As we stood in front of that giant aircraft, all I could visualize was the movie, *Midnight Express.*

We stood on the tarmac for about a half an hour. Finally, we were told to board the aircraft one at a time. We were checked against our passports, which were handed back to us individually. I was glad when the wheels lifted off of Soviet ground.

There were heart-wrenching moments during those jaunts, too. When we were at sea off the coast of Beirut, we missed midnight mass. Bob rarely did that because he'd apparently made a promise to Dolores on those Christmas trips that he'd always attend midnight mass. He couldn't on that Christmas Eve, though, because the bishop who had flown out to say the mass, got seasick. There was no midnight mass.

Bob, Barney McNulty, and I stayed in the Captain's Quarters to work on script changes. The Captain came in and asked if we'd like some Christmas music on while we worked. He slipped a tape in and the first song we heard was Bing Crosby singing "White Christmas." None of us spoke for a bit. I glanced up and noticed tears running down the cheeks of both Bob and McNulty.

Bob liked to take a walk before bedtime. On the ship, we often went out on deck to stroll around. One night, we tried, but the Captain would not permit it. There was no moon and we could have no outside lights. He was afraid that people would trip over the guide wires and such that were all over the deck. Bob had to have his walk, so we roamed around the innards of the USS Guam.

He wandered into one darkened room at about one o'clock in the morning, and then he noticed that it was the hospital ward. We quickly exited, not wanting to wake any of the sick or injured. We got about twenty yards along the corridor when a guy on crutches came chasing after us calling out "Hey, Bob." He insisted that we come back. Bob said he didn't want to wake the guys, but that guy said,

"They're all awake waiting for you." Bob went back in and did about ten minutes of ad-libs.

Bob's casts and crews weren't the only ones who were souvenir hunting. Many of the guys in our troupe worked on various television shows and movies, and they had T-shirts, jackets, and hats that promoted the shows. In Saudi Arabia, we were all on our bus preparing to leave a show that we'd just completed. One of our guys had a T-shirt from some movie. A soldier standing outside said, "Hey, man, I love your shirt." The crew member took off his jacket, whipped off the T-shirt, and threw it out the window to the soldier.

The soldier responded by pulling out a large knife. He took the knife and tore at the stitching that held some patches onto his uniform. He ripped those patches off and handed them in the window to the guy who just gave him the shirt.

I looked out the window at the soldier and saw that tears were streaming down his face. He noticed me noticing him and said to me, "That's the only present I'll be giving anybody this Christmas."

I mentioned earlier that our midnight mass was cancelled on Christmas Eve, but I went to all the religious services they held on board ship that day. There was a non-sectarian service on the hanger deck, and there was a Catholic mass celebrated early in the evening in the forecastle.

It was a small gathering because most of the people had planned on attending the midnight service. Several of us stood there in the bowels of the ship, surrounded by anchor chains. The links of these chains were about four feet high. It was an interesting venue for a religious service.

At one point, the priest invited the participants to "offer each other the sign of peace." I turned to shake hands with the people around me and the first one I greeted was a young marine with an automatic weapon slung across his back. I shook his hand and said, "Peace be with you."

I had done that many times before, but I think that was the first time I really appreciated the meaning of the word, "Peace."

Producer, Eliot Kozak, and I at the Berlin Wall near Checkpoint Charlie.

Director, Tim Kiley , I, and other crew members trying
to find a comfortable seat on our way home from the
around the World Peacetime trip.

(L. to R.) Producer, Eliot Kozak, Gene Perret, Bob Hope, and Lee
Greenwood sharing a laugh on the way to the Persian Gulf. I don't
think the joke we're laughing at made it into the script.

Bob Hope performing at Templehoff Air Base in Berlin.

The entire Bob Hope Troupe posing on the stage at
Rhein Main AFB near Frankfurt, Germany.

Chapter Twenty-Four
Stars

Some writer once said of our profession, "We aren't in show business. We work for people who are in show business."

In a sense, he was right. Stars drive the entertainment business. They put the fannies in the seats. They attract the audience, sell the sponsors' products, and generate the profits.

My writing partner, Bill Richmond, and I had a meeting with Bob Hope at his house in Toluca Lake. It was a beautiful, sprawling home that covered several acres and we sat by a bay window that overlooked the gorgeously manicured back yard with a large swimming pool and golf hole for some quick, free time practicing.

Bob told us about his early days in radio. He used to play golf with a gentleman who owned a company that made boxes for his sponsor's product. The sponsor was a pharmaceutical company that was young then, but became very successful. That guy kept begging off the regular golfing date. When Bob asked him why, he said, "I can't get away. We're too busy at the plant."

Bob said to his agent, "We're making money for this company. They wouldn't be ordering so many boxes if they weren't selling a lot of product. Get me a nice contract."

The agent approached the sponsors and came back to Bob with

the offer of partial ownership in the company. Bob said, "Get me money."

Then, he said to us, "Can you imagine if I had taken a percentage of that company as payment back then?"

Bill Richmond looked around the palatial home and said, "Gee, Bob, you could have been on easy street today."

The stars know they're stars, too.

One time, my wife and I were going go out for dinner. Our four youngsters were just reaching that age where they could be left at home without a baby sitter, yet we felt uncomfortable about it.

Before leaving, I told the kids that if anyone called, they shouldn't say that Mommy and Daddy were out. I instructed them to say that Daddy was in the shower, and then take a number where we could call back.

While we were at dinner, Bob Hope called from New Orleans. When he asked for me, my daughter, Terry, dutifully told him that I was in the shower and asked if I could call back.

Bob said, "I need him right now. Tell him this is Bob Hope calling. He'll get out of the shower for me."

My daughter had no alternate plan. She didn't know what to do, so she hung up.

When I got home, she gave me the message and I called Bob's hotel in New Orleans. We talked for a while, and then he gave me my writing assignment, and asked, "Who was that who answered the phone earlier?"

I said, "That was my daughter."

He said, "Have a talk with your daughter and tell her that I'm a big star. You don't hang up on big stars."

I mentioned earlier that when Bill Richmond and I co-produced *Welcome Back, Kotter,* we inherited many problems that had been going on between the star and the executive producer for some time. We were in the middle between Jimmy Komack and Gabe Kaplan, the star of the series. Kaplan resisted anything we did because he felt we were just shills for Komack.

When the situation became unbearable, we issued an ultimatum that either the star of the show or our producing team would have to go. The people in charge opted to keep our producing squad. Gabe appeared only at the beginning and the end of each show. He was not part of the main storyline.

Shortly afterwards, Gabe went to the network and demanded a hefty raise for each episode . . . and got it.

That's the power that stars have.

I saw another example of star power while working on *Welcome Back, Kotter.* John Travolta was one of the biggest stars in film when we came on as Kotter producers. He was riding high on the crest of two major film roles, *Saturday Night Fever* and *Grease.*

We wanted him to do the show that year, but we weren't sure we could get him. He either was too busy to do the weekly series, or he didn't want to. He wanted to meet the new producing team before he would make a decision. After the meeting, he agreed to do seven to ten episodes. That agreement was a major coup for our producing and writing staff.

John was a delight to work with and he enjoyed doing comedy. He did it well. However, Travolta did something interesting when we worked with him. I was never sure whether it was an innocent failing or done by design. It was a form of upstaging.

At the table reading for the first show that John appeared in, he could just about read the script. He had trouble with the script throughout the week of rehearsals. John was well-liked and all the other cast members helped him.

Then on Friday night, when the cameras were turned on, Travolta was perfect. The rest were a little less prepared. They had spent so much time helping him they had neglected their own rehearsing.

Stars are the glamour of the business, and meeting and working with them is memorable. Memorable for us, that is; not necessarily for them.

John Wayne was once a guest on *Laugh-In* while I worked there. Some stars are even celebrities among celebrities. Bob Hope was, and so was Frank Sinatra. John Wayne was in that class, too.

While I was on the stage watching a sketch being prepared, John held out his hand to me and said, "Hi. I'm John Wayne." I was thrilled. I shook his hand and said, "Gene Perret. I'm one of the writers on the show."

Just then, the director called for quiet as they taped that particular segment. John and I stood side by side and watched the performance. All the while, I kept thinking, *wow, John Wayne introduced himself to me and knows who I am.*

Then, the sketch ended and we were free to talk again.

John Wayne turned to me, held out his hand to me, and said, "Hi. I'm John Wayne."

So much for us being memorable to them.

Working with the stars wasn't always pleasant. In fact, working with the non-stars, pseudo-stars, and "I think I'm a star but nobody agrees with me yet's" wasn't always pleasant, either.

Several of us writers and producers were meeting to cast a show we were planning called *Hallzapoppin*. We were searching for two stars to handle the hosting chores, the roles that Olson and Johnson played on Broadway.

There were two Los Angeles disc jockeys that had a current, hot comedy record. We thought we'd interview them to see if they might host the show. When they came to the interview, they were arrogant.

They walked into the room and turned us down immediately. They said, "You can't write the kind of comedy that we like to do. This show is beneath us. Besides that, you can't afford us." With that, they left.

We were all stunned.

A minute later, there was a knock on the door. The two DJ's who we "couldn't afford" poked their heads back inside, held up their ticket from the parking lot, and said, "Do you guys validate?"

Sometimes the stars would surprise us in a pleasant way. Glen Campbell was performing on a special we did in Sweden. We were in an old theatre, which could have presented logistic problems, and we were working with a foreign stage crew. When Glen was preparing to rehearse his song, they couldn't get a cord to his electric guitar.

Glen was quite relaxed about it. He said, "I'll use my other guitar." For some reason, they couldn't get that to work either.

They tried several alternative plans, but none of them seemed to work. It looked like a major brouhaha would develop.

Campbell said, "It's no problem. I'll do the song without a guitar."

That was a perfect opportunity for a star to throw a tantrum. Instead, Glen remained calm and solved the problem without incident.

As an aside, Glen provided a memorable evening of entertainment during that trip. Several of us visited the hotel lounge after work that night. A musician played piano and guitar and sang some songs in the lounge. Glen asked if he could play the guitar and join in the music.

Glen played and sang for a couple of hours that evening. It was great music and great fun.

I told Glen how interested I was in guitar music and we spoke of Django Reinhart quite a bit that night. After the trip, Glen sent me a group of records that included all of Django Reinhart's recorded music.

Tony Randall was always a consummate professional, who brought unbridled enthusiasm and 110% effort to whatever project he was working on. He brought tremendous energy to any stage he was on.

He used a trick that was delightful during the tapings. Often, someone or another flubbed a line during taping and we had to go back and pick up the shooting. Whoever the culprit was had to cover for the mistake and apologize to the audience.

Tony Randall, before a performance, announced to the audience that he had been in show business many, many years, and in all that time, he had never flubbed a line during a performance. He emphasized the "never."

Then, of course, if he did blow a line during the taping, the audience got a tremendous kick out of it. It seemed clever of him to buy his own "insurance policy" before the taping even began.

He was a guest on a show we did from Florida one year. Again, it was when Bob Hope's concentration was failing. Bob and Tony Randall were to do a song number. It was a copy of a song that he and Bing Crosby had done in one of their road pictures. The song was called "Apalachacola."

As a guide, we had a tape of the Hope-Crosby routine from the film. Each time they rehearsed, Bob got either the lyrics or the dance steps wrong. He blamed it on Randall.

They watched the tape, which showed that Randall, was perfect, but Bob was off. Bob, though, insisted that he had done the routine correctly and Randall hadn't.

That was repeated time and time again. The rehearsal went on for hours. Throughout this ordeal, though, Randall never defended himself and never accused Bob of being wrong. Instead, he endured with a calm, pleasant attitude out of respect for Bob.

It was an inspiring rehearsal to watch.

Whether working with the stars was pleasant or unpleasant, it was always fascinating. Those folks were exciting.

I remember how thrilled I was when Neil Armstrong was scheduled to appear on one of the Bob Hope specials. I was looking forward to meeting and working with the man who first stepped on the moon.

However, when I showed up for work, things began to appear ominous. One stagehand was sweeping up the stage and when he saw me he said, "Boy, you'd better run and hide. Things aren't going so well around here."

Then, I saw a couple of the cue card guys who said, "You'd better straighten things out with Neil Armstrong before Hope shows up."

One of the NBC guys told me, "You'd better grab a script and smooth things over with Neil Armstrong. He's furious."

None of them would tell me what was wrong.

Reluctantly, I took my script into Neil Armstrong's dressing room. I introduced myself and said, "I understand you have a problem with the script."

"Yes, I do," he said.

"Maybe we can fix it," I said.

"Sure," he said. "There are just a few minor problems."

In our script, we had called his trip to the moon a "perfect flight." He pointed out, though, that there had been something like 237 flaws during the journey. Those were technical problems by NASA standards, not major problems.

There were a few other errors with the technical wording of the piece. They were things an astronaut would want to be precise about, but a comedy writer might not.

Together, Neil and I corrected the script in about five or six minutes. Neil was polite and cooperative, and all the rumors I heard on my way into the studio were just that—exaggerated rumors.

A similar thing happened when Roseanne Barr (as she was known then) was scheduled to appear on the Bob Hope show. Everyone assumed she would be a terror. She had a reputation for being tough with the staff and crew on her own sitcom. We figured it would carry over to our show, but she was absolutely no trouble. She read the lines, took direction, and accepted changes, all without resistance . . . until the day of taping.

Right before the taping, she called me over as head-writer and said very politely, "You know there's one line here I don't understand." She pointed it out to me and it was an error in the printing of the script. She had a punch line to a setup that no longer existed. It had been removed in the final typing.

I went back and got some earlier scripts and penciled in the correct joke, which Roseanne liked. That problem was easily solved.

Then, Roseanne said to me, "Thank you very much. But here's another joke that I think stinks." It looks harsh on paper, but she said it in a kidding way.

The writers worked on it and came up with a new line that she accepted before the cameras were turned on.

She handled the changes correctly, politely, and with a sense of humor.

We had another script problem with a star that looked like it was going to be trouble, but it wasn't. Brooke Shields had been a guest on the Bob Hope show so many times that it got to be an industry joke. She was always bright, cheerful, prepared as an actress, and a pleasure to be around. That's why it was such a shock when she complained that she couldn't do what the script required her to do.

"What's the problem?" I asked

Brooke said, "I just can't do this."

"Why not?" I asked.

"It's impossible," she told me.

Of course, we writers girded up to defend our script and all of the jokes in it. We thought that stars were too demanding and always asked for special treatment and so on and so forth.

"What's impossible about it?" I asked.

Brooke said, "This scene right here. I have three entrances and only one exit."

She was right—it was impossible.

What happened was that Bob Hope had taken various versions of the sketch that the writers had turned in to him separately. That was his way of preparing the scripts. He marked off different sections from those several drafts that he thought were funny and then combined them into one sketch. It turned out in that final version that Brooke was supposed to make an entrance or two when she was already on stage.

We rewrote the script so that she would only have to come onto the set if she wasn't already there. She was pleasant in pointing out the error to us and continued to be a delight through the rest of the show.

It wasn't always as easy as it was with Roseanne and Brooke, though. Burt Reynolds appeared on the Bob Hope shows many times. For some reason on one particular show, he was not happy with the way things were going. I had no idea what the problem was, but it was obvious to all of us on the stage that there was a problem.

I had to take some script changes into Burt's dressing room and review them with him before the next scene was taped. He invited me in, but he was not pleased with any of the changes. He accepted them and approved them, but was surly about it.

All I wanted to do was get the changes okayed and onto cue cards before he started taking things out on me personally. When we got the last line changed and approved, I was eager to exit. I really enjoyed his new television show, *Evening Shade,* and I was going to tell him that before I left. If he wanted to get sore at me for that, fine.

"I really think you're new show is superb," I said.

"Thank you," he said.

I said, "I think the writing is great and you've got a fantastic cast."

"They're all friends," he said, "who did me a favor."

I said, "Well, I just wanted to tell you that," as I edged toward the door.

"Sit down," he said, "You don't have to rush out, do you?"

Whatever was bothering him until then disappeared. We had a pleasant conversation about his show, and all the changes on our show went into the script with no more problems.

The celebrities could embarrass us at times, too. When Bob Hope was made a "Four Star Hero," I was to write the presentations for the presenters. We had a four star admiral representing the Navy, and four star generals from each of the other branches of the service.

I tried to co-ordinate the writing so that each person would present a portion of the thank you to Bob. I contacted each one of them, reviewed what I was going to write, got their okay on that, and then sent drafts of the script for their notes and final approval. I reached every one of the dignitaries except General William Westmoreland. He was never available.

The first time I met or spoke with General Westmoreland was in the green room immediately before the taping. Of course, I had to write a script before then, which I did. However, when I went into the green room with Bob and the four-star representatives of the military, I asked General Westmoreland if he had received his copy.

He said, "Yes. I don't like it."

I asked why.

He said, "I can't single out this branch of the service to honor. I have to pay tribute to all of them. They all did a great job."

I explained that we were having different presenters honor different branches of the service.

He admitted he wasn't aware of that. *He would have been if he had responded to my phone calls,* I thought.

He said, "I see. I still don't like it."

We were about to tape that segment in about ten minutes, so I said, "General, maybe you would like to make some changes and we can quickly get them on cue cards for you."

He said, "I'd like to do that. Give me a pencil."

I searched my pockets. I had no pencil or pen.

General Westmoreland looked toward Bob. He shrugged and said, "I have the only writers who don't carry writing instruments."

One of the general's aides supplied a pen. We made the changes and incorporated them into the show.

However, Bob was aware of my embarrassment and attempted to bail me out.

After all the changes were made and just before we were about to tape, Bob told Westmoreland about a gag I had written that day.

Our troupe had visited Sea World and had been allowed into the penguin display to pet and touch the birds. Our guide mentioned that penguins are birds with wings, but they don't fly. I wrote a piece that incorporated that information into the show.

A guest mentioned to Bob the fact that penguins don't fly. He responded, "Don't you think it's silly that penguins have wings but they can't fly."

The guest said, "Not really. You have golf clubs."

Bob told the general that story to ease my humiliation over the pencil. I don't think General Westmoreland was impressed.

When I first began to consider making comedy my lifetime profession—back in the late 1950's and early 1960's—I used to send material to Peter Lind Hayes. Hayes and his wife, Mary Healy, were well-known personalities in the early days of television and they had a radio show out of New York. Peter read my submissions, introducing me as "My funny friend from Upper Darby."

I wasn't paid for the material, but felt it would be good practice and worthwhile exposure. After several weeks of that, Peter Lind Hayes sent me a note thanking me for my writing.

He was the first to make my short list of celebrities who thanked me for material.

Bob Hope was on that list often. Bob was a demanding boss, who worked the writers hard. He felt he had that right since he paid his scribes well. However, he was always very gracious in thanking the individual writers for a job well done.

I wrote a special honoring Jimmy Doolittle, the general who master-minded the counter-attack on Tokyo after the Pearl Harbor bombing.

For that show, I wrote a couple of pieces for Jimmy Stewart, who was a general in the Air Force reserves, and for Lee Marvin.

Because I was traveling on speaking engagements, I couldn't be at the taping of that show.

However, a week or two later, I got a phone call. When I answered the phone, I heard a weak, older-sounding voice asking for Gene Perret.

I said, "Who's calling?"

The voice said, "This is Jimmy Stewart."

I said, "This is Gene."

He said, "I just wanted to thank you for that piece you wrote for me for Jimmy Doolittle."

A day or two later, Lee Marvin called with a gracious thank you, too.

Many years later, in 2001, after Bob Hope had retired, Wayne Newton was asked to step into his shoes and do a USO Christmas show for the troops engaged in combat zones around the world. He asked Martha Bolton and me to help out with the comedy.

Wayne also remembered to thank the writers.

That's pretty much the complete list of stars that went out of their way to say "Thank you." I thank all of the stars I've worked with, for, or against for the lifetime of memories they've given me.

To learn more about the craft and profession of comedy writing, read these other books by *Gene Perret*.

The New Comedy Writing Step by Step
(Quill Driver Books, 2007, $14.95)

This is an updated version of *Comedy Writing Step by Step* that was originally published in 1982 and has been the *bible* for comedians and comedy writers ever since. The book is a thorough how-to manual that not only encourages and inspires would be writers, but also guides them step by step through the comedy writing process – from the blank pages to the completed manuscript.

Breakfasts with Archangel Shecky (and His Infallible, Irrefutable, Unassailable, One-Size-Fits-All Secrets of Success) (Quill Driver Books, 2009, $19.95)

This is a fictional story of a young Philadelphian who is struggling to become a recognized standup comedian. Circumstances begin to change for the better when he meets a stranger who calls himself "Archangel Shecky" and claims to be the comic's Guardian Angel.

This angel loves to drink scotch and eat all of the foods that Philly is famous for – cheese steaks, hoagies, soft pretzels, and such. However, he hates to – and refuses to – pick up any bar tabs or restaurant checks.

Yet he offers solid advice on comedy—not just on comedy, though. Also on how to achieve whatever you want in any profession.

Is "Shecky" angelic or is he a dead beat? Is his wisdom valid or simply a ploy to get free scotch? All of these questions are resolved in *Breakfasts with Archangel Shecky.*

Also check Gene Perret's website, www.writingcomedy.com to order these books and to learn more about the e-mail courses he teaches – with personal feedback and critiques – on various aspects of humor writing.

Index:

CPSIA information can be obtained at www.ICGtesting.com
Printed in the USA
LVOW071054161012

303026LV00001B/2/P